Amante
I will Always Love
you. Thank you
for supporting me.
Bless you sis

Kendal S. Turn

Cover design by Austin Nichols

Angel number references by Joanne Walmsley
http://sacredscribesangelnumbers.blogspot.com/

Kendal S. Turner

The Power
of
22

Books by Kendal S. Turner

Broken Yet Sustained by God
Anatomy of the Soul
Epiphany
Thick Skin

Kendal S. Turner website
www.kendalsturnor.com
contact@kendalsturner.com

The Power
of
22

STORIES OF VISIONS, MANIFESTATIONS
& INTUITIVE GUIDANCE

Kendal S. Turner

To my mom, dad and granny.
Thank you for guiding me from the other side. I am grateful for the lessons, wisdom and love that you have given me. I honor you in spirit and in truth. Until we see each other again. RIP. I will always love you.

Introduction

We are not taught to listen to ourselves. We are not trained on how to trust our intuition. Most of us were raised in church with a pastor telling us who we are, and what we can and cannot do or be. We live in a world full of boundaries and rules. Where judging others is much more common, than finding the humility to look inward at ourselves, and find out the truth of who we really are. Before we came into this world, we knew who we were. We knew that we came from divine unconditional love. We knew the gifts that we had and the power that we possessed. Life has beat us down and stripped us to our core of the things that make us unique. So instead of living our truth, we walk around like helpless victims with no power to overcome situations. God has equipped us with spiritual gifts and the power to overcome any obstacle. It is our duty to find out what those gifts are and use them for the betterment of mankind. The power of **22** will do just that!

In this book, I will share with you true stories of visions, manifestations and intuitive guidance. This book speaks to the work of the soul, and shows you how to look inwardly for direction. You will see how every relationship, situation and circumstance is relative to your divine purpose. The power of **22** will inspire you to trust your instincts, and teach you how to manifest the desires of your heart. You will be encouraged to work diligently on your life path, and seek out the truth, of who you really are.

Habakkuk 2:2
And the Lord answered me, and said, write the vision, and make it plain upon tables, that he may run that readeth it. (KJV)

Visions

My son Kory was born on September **22**, 2003. When he was about 6 weeks old, I started having spiritual encounters. I remember feeding him one night around 3am and the weirdest thing happened to me. I was laying down on my stomach and I could feel a presence playing in my hair. It wasn't a gentle twirl of the fingers, it was more of a flipping motion from side to side. I could also hear what sounded like wings flapping in my right ear. Like angel wings fluttering. I woke up shook, not knowing what the hell was going on. As I was sitting up in my bed, my heartbeat was racing 100mph and the hairs on my arm were standing up. The hairs on the back of my neck stood erect. Then I felt a presence stroking the side of my left cheek as if to calm me down. My oldest son was 8 years old at the time, asleep next to me. I looked over at him and as he was asleep, he brushed off his head as if he could feel something crawling on him. He never woke up though. I jumped out of the bed and ran into the bathroom to look in the mirror. Just as I thought, my hair looked just like someone had been playing in it. The back of my hair was all over the place! My son was the catalyst for my spiritual encounters.

There were times when I thought I saw a little baby running through my house. I didn't mention it to my spouse at the time because I knew he didn't understand spiritual things and that wasn't something you just blurted out in mid conversation. "Hey I forgot to tell you there's a baby running through this house." Yea. No. I dismissed the incident as a figment of my imagination.

Months later, when Kory was mobile and able to say a few words, something supernatural happened. He was crawling around the kitchen table. He stopped mid stride, stood up and started looking under the table as if he saw something. I was washing dishes, with my back turned to him, but keeping an eye on him at the same time. I noticed whatever it was he saw, had his undivided attention.

I said to him, "Pooda what do you see?"

He pulled his pacifier out of his mouth, bent down and pointed under the kitchen table.

"Baby" He said.

He put the pacifier back in his mouth and stood staring into space. I knew from that day forward, my son had the gift.

Let me take you back to my childhood so you can have a better understanding of who I am, and why I titled this book *The power of 22*. Stay with me as I show you how **22** has been guiding me my entire life, without me even realizing it. As mentioned in my autobiography *Thick Skin,* I grew up on the north side of Tulsa, Oklahoma. My mother and father had a tumultuous relationship from start to finish. My father was **22** years old when I was birthed into this world. I was the only good thing that came from their union. I am proof that there is purpose in every relationship. My home address was **2022** from the 3rd grade until graduating from high school. After graduating from Booker T. Washington Highschool, I attended Dillard University in New Orleans, La. The zip code is **70122**.

By the age of 24, I had given birth to 2 sons; Courtland and Kory. After a failed marriage to their father in 2004, I remarried just six months after my divorce was final in 2005. As you can see I wasted no time moving on. Instead of taking the time to examine myself and the poor decisions I made thus far, I just kept it moving. Carrying baggage from one relationship to the next. (You can order *Thick Skin* if you want to know more about all that drama). My second marriage was to a guy who was my best friend at the time. I sold my house in Tulsa and moved to Oklahoma City to be with him. I used the profit from the sale of my Tulsa home to buy us a house in Oklahoma City. The zip code for that house is **73122**. I swear I can't make this stuff up!

In 2012, after 7 years of marriage, we decided to go our separate ways. When you build a life with someone, there are certain luxuries you become accustomed to. Like having two incomes and a support system. I can honestly say that during my second marriage, I dropped the ball in my prayer life because he was stronger in that area than I was. He would get up every morning at 5am to pray for us. I on the other hand, slacked horribly. I would go days without praying. It wasn't until we separated that I took the reins on my prayer life because I was made to be the head of the house.

I had to reorganize my finances. I changed banks, re-routed my direct deposits and reduced the amount of money I had going into my 401k. I took him off my car insurance to reduce the monthly payment. I took him off my cell phone bill to lower that bill too. I took him off everything we shared together in hopes to have a more affordable life for me and my kids. As time progressed, worry set in, and I wondered if I made the right decision. n the outside looking in, I appeared to have it all together. I never had a meltdown. I never let anyone see me without a smile on my face. I had this unwavering faith that everything would be okay even when it didn't always feel like it. It's almost as if the power of **22** was sustaining me. There I was in this three-bedroom house that went from a family of **6** to a family of **3**. I was miserable in my marriage, and the only reason we were together for 7 years, was my fear of being where I eventually ended up anyway. Alone with no help. At least I thought I had no help.

On **3-22-2012**, amid trying to get my life back in order, I had a dream. I dreamt I was in a room with other people, but I was laying down on my back, in the middle of a crowded room. In the corner was a big lion. I saw him pacing the floor slowly but no one else seemed to see the lion but me. He was big like the lion king! The lion walked over to me, stood over me and started speaking! He said, "the devil comes to kill, steal and destroy." Then he named all the people in the bible who were destroyed by the devil.

He continued, "But for you, if you have debts, pay them. If you have loans, pay them. The next time you go to the store, get exactly what you need."
He walked off then came back over to me. I was terrified. His voice was so powerful it resonated through my entire being. This lion put his face close to my face and breathed on me. His breath alone was powerful enough to make your eyelashes fall off. It was like wind blowing on my

face. I was trembling with fear until I realized he meant me no harm. I woke up. God was reassuring me. I got you...

By this time, my oldest son decided he wanted to move back to Tulsa with his dad. His dad convinced him that he could help him make the basketball team down there, so I went against my better judgement and let him go anyway. He was in high school, and I knew at that age he needed his dad more than he needed me. Even though I knew that move would set him back a few years. Now it was just me and Kory in this 3-bedroom house all alone.

It seemed like once everybody was out of the house, whatever spiritual connection that me and Kory had magnified. Almost as if there was no more spiritual interference. It was like we had a laser force contact with heaven. He was seeing things. I was seeing things. He was getting the cold feeling and I was getting hot. If you could be a fly on the wall, people would think we was losing our minds. When I was married I would have dreams and visitations but when I would tell my spouse about it, he would make fun of me. This caused me to keep quiet about my experiences because I didn't have anyone to validate me or believe me. I was lonely in my marriage.

Remember the little baby that I saw when Kory was just a few months old? Well that baby followed me to Oklahoma City. I remember a time when my ex-husband was in the bathroom and I was laying in the bed.

"Uh honey" he said.

"Yes"

"The toilet tissue just unraveled by itself."

I giggled, "Its ok honey it's just the baby messing with you."

"I don't know what kinda woman I married."
Since he made fun of me, I stopped telling him stuff all together. I on purpose didn't tell him about the visitation I had with the little baby one night. I can remember so vividly sleeping peacefully. Our bedroom was pitch black and I felt this tap on my left shoulder. Like someone poked me. I thought it was Kory cause at the time he was still small. I opened my eyes and I could see the silhouette of a little boy standing in front of me, about knee high. I said, "what Kory." There was silence. I rubbed my eyes and realized no one was there. So, to make sure I wasn't tripping, I got up to go check Kory's bed. He was still asleep. All the doors were locked and no one else was awake. I know I saw a little boy standing in front of me. I kept that visitation to myself because I didn't want to be made fun of.

My son and I established our new normal. After the dust settled from the divorce, I was able to pay all my bills and establish a new routine for us. Everything was okay. I was over it! A year later, on March 15th, 2013, my spiritual ear kicked into overdrive. Around 10:45pm my cousin called but I didn't answer the phone because I wasn't in the mood to talk. I figured if it was important, she would leave me a voicemail and I would check it when I woke up. Around 4 am as I was sound asleep, I heard a baby crying. I also heard a woman's voice trying to calm the baby. It was a muffled moaning sound, but I am for certain it was a woman's voice. The babies cry grew louder and louder to the point where I sat up in the bed, trying to figure out where the sound was coming from. It's like it was in my inner ear if that makes any sense. I jumped out of bed and put my ear to the bedroom window, thinking maybe somebody is on the side of my house. Now, my neighborhood consisted of old Caucasian people. All of my neighbors were in their 90's and barely alive, let alone having babies. I knew the noise wasn't coming from their house, but I couldn't figure out where it was coming from. I put my ear to the wall then to the floor vent. Still nothing! So, I got up and walked down the hallway. I could still hear the baby crying! I checked the back door, nothing was there. I looked out the front door. Nothing was there. I checked Kory's room and he was sound asleep. Where is this baby?! Then it stopped. Then there was silence.

I went back into my bedroom, shut the door and sat up in my bed, dazed and confused. What in the world just happened? Was I hearing things? Its 4am, where is this baby that I know I heard? Eventually I fell back asleep and was woken up by my alarm at 6am. I woke Kory up and started getting ready for work. He was complaining about his stomach hurting. I thought maybe he needed a bowel movement, so I told him to see if he can poop.

"Mom my stomach hurts really bad."

"Okay well go drink some water Kory."

"But mom it hurts."

"I don't know what you want me to do if you can't poop."

I dismissed his stomach pain and made him get ready for school. I thought for certain he was trying to get out of going to school like most kids do. Boy was I wrong.

I dropped Kory off at school and headed to work. There was nothing different about my drive. The sun was coming up. I had my 7-11 coffee and traffic was flowing smoothly. So far so good. I made it to work on time and followed my usual routine. I sat there for about 30 minutes sipping my coffee and checking emails. Then the phone rang. It was my cousin again.

"Hey" she said.

"Hey, what's going on?"

"Where are you?"

"I'm at work."

"I have some bad news about your dad."

"What?"

"Your dad was in a car accident last night and he didn't make it."

There was a long pause. I honestly didn't know what to say. I was at work and couldn't cry. I didn't know how to feel because my dad and I weren't on the best terms. I hadn't spoken to him in a while, but I wasn't angry with him. We just weren't talking.

"I knew something was going on because I heard a baby crying." I replied.

"sigh."

We sat on the phone for a while, not really knowing what to say. After hanging up the phone, I called my momma and told her that daddy had passed away. She busted out crying and hung up in my face. I didn't know nothing about planning a funeral. My daddy lived in Tulsa and I was an hour ½ away in Oklahoma City. Eventually I got ahold of the funeral home and everything was set in motion. I received a copy of the police report that showed my daddy driving on the highway, veering off at a high rate of speed, and eventually crashing into a tree. He was not wearing a seat belt, so his head went through the windshield. Apparently, he fell asleep at the wheel. I was told that he broke both legs from the thigh on down. The impact from the steering wheel severed his liver in half.

He had multiple abdominal injuries. When I saw the report, it dawned on me that my son felt the impact of my daddy's injuries. I felt bad for dismissing my son but from a human standpoint, how was I supposed to know this boy was an empath? I had never heard of such a thing. He was only in the 4th grade and kids make stuff up all the time. I do know that would be the last time I ever dismissed his feelings. They say whenever a person dies, a baby is born. I believe the baby that I heard in my spiritual ear was the birth of a new life coming into this world.

Not even a month later, my son and I had a craving for some Braums cheeseburgers and ice cream. We decided to dine in since the drive through was packed. We ordered our meal and waited for our ticket to be called. As we sat in the booth, I noticed a Mexican man sitting in the booth across the way. He was drinking a chocolate shake, sitting there with a neck brace on, minding his own business. I assume he was in a car accident. Anyway, I didn't think much of it. They called my number, so I ran up to get our food. As we were eating, I noticed Kory kept looking over at the man.

"Mom I can feel that mans pain."

"What man?"

"The man with the neck thingy on."

"What do you mean you can feel his pain?"

"My neck hurts really bad mom. I can feel that man's pain."

I believed him. I wondered how a 4th grader could even rationalize the idea of feeling someone else's pain, without ever hearing someone speak of such a thing. He could have just said his own neck hurt. The fact that he related the pain he was feeling, to being someone else's

17

and not his own was baffling to me. I didn't know what to say or do. I didn't have any spiritual people around me to teach me how to deal with my gift let alone my child's. I don't find it a coincidence that God would bless me with a child who is my mirror. I believe Kory is one of my soulmates. Maybe we were together in a past life or something. He is the spitting image of me. Being who I am has also prepared me for knowing how to parent my son. I can see why he chose me to be his mother.

The house was becoming too much for me to manage with the utilities, yard work and maintenance repairs. I just didn't want the hassle anymore and we didn't need all that space. When I would take my Camaro to the dealership for an oil change, I would pass by the Links apartments on NW 122ND ST. I stopped by the office one day to see if I could get a tour of the apartments and the lady indulged me. I instantly fell in love with the place. I needed to find an apartment with rent that was cheaper than my mortgage payment, so I could save money. So, before I looked at those apartments, I made a list of amenities I wanted in my new place. I wrote down a rent payment of less than $725 a month. I needed two bathrooms and a washer and drier hookup. After the lady gave me a tour, I sat down with her to discuss the price ranges for the two bedrooms. She said the rent would be $750 but since they had a waiting list, I had to wait.

I put my house up for sale and prayed daily that a vacancy would come available. I must have called that office every Friday to check the status of availability. I called so much they knew me by name. I would drive through the complex at night to see if it was quiet. I would drive through there on my lunch break to see if people were hanging out in the parking lot. I was borderline obsessed with that apartment. I fell in love with it.

Finally, one day the lady called me and said she had a vacancy but there was one problem. It was a handicap unit. It was the same size as the one I looked at. It was facing the golf course which means it was in the back. That meant it was quiet! I jumped for joy. She said there was nothing different about that apartment except for the bathroom had handrails in it. I did not care! Oh, and get this. She said since it's a handicap apartment, I would get $50 off rent. My rent would be $700! Praise God! Not to mention, it came with a washer and drier! Yassssssss. God is in the blessing business and I was ready to receive it baby!

We moved into that apartment in 2013 and Kory loved it just as much as I did. Things were so much better for us over there. No more yards to cut. No more repairs to make. No more utilities! Man, I was living the life, you hear me. I had money to spend and enough left over to put into savings. Things were starting to look up for the kid. I got exactly what I asked for. I made a request to God. I wrote down my list of wishes and God answered. Ask and it is Given.

A year passed by and everything was smooth sailing. I was focused on my poetry gigs and speaking engagements. I had a side hustle selling bowties. I was selling everything from hats, socks, bracelets and scarves. You name it, I had it! I made $5k in one month just off my side hustle. Life was good. But we all know how God works right? As soon as we get comfortable, he throws a rod in our plan. Later on in the year, I noticed my gigs started drying up. I have performed at over 150 churches in

Oklahoma alone. I performed at every open mic spot. I did plays, women conferences, youth events and some colleges. I am a well-known poet in my hometown. I was one of the most sought-after poets. I was the poet on speed dial. It was like overnight, my phone just stopped ringing. I thought what in the world is going on? When I tell you, I went from being booked to questioning my purpose in life, I was confused. I knew something spiritual was happening I just didn't understand it. Divine destiny was happening and like a title wave it took over my life swiftly.

January 13, 2014 started off like a normal wintery cold day in Oklahoma City, Oklahoma. My son and I left the house around 6:45am to drop him off at school on the other side of town. As I drove under the Broadway extension bridge to get in the left-hand lane, we came to a complete stop due to heavy traffic. My son had his iPad in hand, head hung low, immersed in some YouTube video about motorcycles. He was always quiet on the way to school so it was nothing out of the ordinary for us. Then out of nowhere, without even looking up, my son says,
"mom I think you need to look for a new job."
At the time he was in the 5th grade. He knew nothing about the hustle and bustle of the corporate world nor did he know how much money I was making at the time. However; because I knew my son and the infinite wisdom he had, I knew he must have known something that I didn't.
"Why would I look for a new job Kory? I like my job."
Again, without looking up, he shrugs his shoulders and says, "I don't know." I looked at him in confusion.

I've called him my little prophet ever since he was a baby. He had a way about him. His eyes are pure and honest. I used to tell my friends, when Kory speaks, I listen. Still unsure of what prompted him to say that I asked,

"Why did you say that Kory?"

"I don't know mom."

Without any further explanation, he buried his head in the iPad and resumed to watching YouTube. The prophet had spoken.

I made it to work around 7:45am. I hadn't thought any more or less about what Kory said to me. I had been working at that job for 12 years. It required little or no thinking what so ever. I was just going through the motions yet not complaining about how much my job sucked simply because of the money I was making. I was a single parent. My checks were usually around $900 every two weeks. I was able to pay all my bills, go shopping when I wanted to and eat out every day. Changing jobs was nowhere on my list of things to do. I was comfortable and unfulfilled at the same time.

Every day was like the day before. I would sit for about 30 minutes with a black screen on my monitor and sip my coffee from 7-11. Log into twitter and tweet my daily affirmations. Post a status on Facebook or just sit there and talk to my co-workers before I did any work. My job did not challenge me mentally. It didn't require me to be great. I wasn't changing the world or making a positive impact on society. All I did was click the mouse and grade work orders. I was slowly dying at that job.

Coincidently, my work husband rolled his chair into my little cubical and started giving me a rundown of the latest gossip.

"You know they talking about laying off don't you," He says.

"You know I don't keep up with all that mess."

"Well I heard they are doing away with some of the departments and sending jobs to Las Vegas and Atlanta." He says with his eyebrows raised.

"Oh well, God got me."

He was a worry wort. He stressed about the littlest things and never had faith in any situation. He wasn't very spiritual at all so I was constantly on him about staying positive and trusting the process.

We rolled our chairs back into our respective cubes and proceeded with our boring day. I couldn't help but think about what Kory told me earlier that morning.

"Mom I think you need to find a new job."

On February 11, 2014 I dreamt I was at a park with my co-workers. It seemed like a company picnic and all of a sudden, the clouds turned dark. I told someone a storm is coming. I asked what direction is the storm going and they said Northeast, which was the same direction I was going. I was on my bike but I couldn't decide whose house I was going over since the storm was headed in my direction. I remember riding my bike fast but there were a lot of other bikers as well. All of us were trying to beat the storm. We drove through a pile of poop and it was sticky and stinky. Piles and piles of poop everywhere. I woke up. I knew that my life was about to get real and fast. My son warned me first. Then my co-worker then my dream. God always confirms his word but it is up to us to heed the warnings.

For a month, the employee morale was low without any tangible evidence of a threat to anyone's job. Based solely on he said-she said, people were downright depressed. I on the other hand, took comfort in knowing that God had warned me ahead of time and confirmed his word with me. All I could do was plan for the worst but only speak positive about the situation. Whenever someone came to me worrying and crying, I just listened and replied, "everything will be okay."

On March 5, 2014 our supervisor called for a mandatory meeting. Here we go. We sat around the long cherry wood round table, in this cold room with two doors and chalk board. She came in with a manila folder looking disheveled. With bags under her eyes, hair looking like it hadn't been combed in days, she busted out in tears.

"Guys many of you have already heard, Cox is doing some restructuring. This is not just going to affect Oklahoma but it's a regional reconstruction so this will impact 5,000 people." She cried. The room was cold and silent. Not one word was spoken. You could literally feel the energy of fear bouncing off the person sitting next to you.

"Our entire department is being laid off." She said. But here's the kicker. Not only did they lay us off but they wanted us to continue working until May 5th. That meant we had to work for 2 months knowing we didn't have a job. People were calling in and applying for jobs online. They even tried to help us in our job search by providing us with a resume writing class. I didn't do either one. I didn't look for a job. I didn't call in. I didn't cry or have a pity party. I walked out of that room with my head held high because I knew that all would be well.

Reflecting on the dream I had of the company picnic. There was a lot of us on bikes trying to get away from the tornado. This was the 5,000 people who were laid off. Little did I know; the piles of poop would be symbolic of all the crap I was about to go through.

My severance packaged consisted of 6 weeks of pay and I could file for unemployment for 6 months. I had $22,000 in my 401k that I didn't plan on touching until my other resources dried up. I'm pretty good with money management so I knew that I had at least 1 ½ years to get my life together before I had to go back to work.

My earlobes started to heat up for no reason. I tried to relate it to maybe good things coming to me or my angels being present, but I had no definite explanation. I do remember them heating up one day at work right before I clocked out. I took Kory to the barbershop on Western and Hefner. While Kory was in the chair, I received an unexpected phone call. The barbershop was noisy, so I took the conversation outside. It was my cousin calling to tell me that my granny had passed away. I sat outside the barbershop in tears. Kory didn't see me cry nor did he hear my phone call from outside. My granny was my #1 fan. We would talk on the phone for hours at a time. I didn't know how I was going to break the news to Kory. Even though he hadn't spent much time with her, he knew who she was. I had to figure out a way to tell him.

We left the barbershop and grabbed a bite to eat. I was quiet all the way home thinking about my granny. When we finally made it home, Kory went to his room as he always did, and I sat in the living room. After working up the nerve to tell him, I sat down next to him on his bunk bed.

"Kory I need to tell you something," I said.

He put his iPad down and gazed at me with his bright brown eyes.

"Is it granny? Did she die?"

My eyes bucked.

"How did you know?"

"I don't know."

He stood up in front of me and leaned over to kiss me on my forehead.

"Its okay mom. She's in a better place."

Still shocked that this little boy already knew before I told him. Not only that, he had shown me so much compassion and reassurance that she was okay. Somehow, he knew exactly what I needed. I stood up and he hugged me so tight. Then he sat back down on his bunk bed, and proceeded to play in his iPad as if nothing happened. He didn't shed one tear.

The last time I spoke to my granny was two weeks before she passed. She told me that she was tired of burying her kids. "I'm tired Kendal," she told me. My granny buried three of her five sons before she passed. I truly believe when the soul is ready to transition, it will. I believe we know when our time has come. I believe that we choose when we are ready to go. My granny died from a broken heart. She just couldn't take it any longer.

About two weeks after granny passed, as I was asleep, I felt someone kiss me on my forehead. I could feel her presence in my room and I instantly knew it was her. I woke up crying uncontrollably. I was crying in my sleep. My granny had visited me to let me know that all is well.

The last week on the job, I was cleaning out my desk and putting everything in boxes, so I wouldn't have to succumb to the humiliation, of having to walk out with boxes on the last day. By this time, nobody was being productive. We basically said screw this job and didn't do any more work. Luckily, they started outsourcing our work to other departments, so we didn't have much to do anyway. As I was cleaning out my desk, I felt a hand on my right shoulder. I thought it was my work husband because he was always in a talkative mood. I turned around and no one was there. Thinking maybe he was hiding, I peeked over the cubical wall and he wasn't in his cube. As a matter of fact, no one was in the room. I know I wasn't tripping. I know I felt a hand on my shoulder, but no one was there. I believe it was a visitation from my granny.

The last day of work was a very emotional day for us. I personally didn't cry, but most of the women in my department did. Some were more spiritually grounded than others. They were crying in the hallway. Hugging each other and having nervous breakdowns. People outside with boxes in their hands. We exchanged phone numbers and some of us became Facebook friends now that we wouldn't be working together. I worked for Cox for 12 years and most of my co-workers had been there longer than I. Some 15, 17 even 20 years long. All of that came to a screeching halt on May 5th, 2014. We lost our health insurance, our stability and some people lost their sanity. Can you imagine building a stable life for your family, only for it to be ripped from underneath you in an instant? I was a single parent with no outside financial support. No child support, no social security, no welfare. Nothing. If ever there was a time that I needed reassurance that God would not fail me, the time is NOW. The hand that I felt on my shoulder, was Gods tangible expression of unconditional love whispering, "I got you."

Manifestations

After getting laid off, I started reading books on the law of attraction and the laws of the universe. That eventually led me to books about angels, meditation, number sequences, signs, synchronicity and energy. I figured if I was going to be unemployed, instead of looking for a new job, I would take this time to do some work on myself. I read a total of 9 books dealing with spirituality and self-awareness. We are only as strong as our mind, and to make it through this transition I needed to get grounded spiritually. I had no more time to waste.

In my quest for spiritual enlightenment, I read up on meditation and that's when my life went from black and white to high definition. It's like my six senses opened. I could feel more. Colors became brighter. My sense of smell was magnified and my spiritual eyes opened. I started to feel a magnetic energy around me. I started feeling other people's emotions and pain. If someone was sad around me, then I became sad. If your knee was aching, then my knee would ache. My mind was sharp. My thinking became clear. My intuition increased dramatically. It made me calmer and more compassionate. When everything around me seemed chaotic, I was at peace. Meditation helped me to be present and in the moment. I started hearing angels talk to me in my right ear. I could sense when someone else was in the room with me. My communication with the other side magnified. Although I've always had spiritual gifts, meditation seemed to open me up and it increased what gifts I already had. Little did I know this was all a part of Gods plan. I felt like I was walking around blind folded with only my spirit to guide me. It was a scary time for me, yet the more experiences I had the deeper I dove. I'm like a sponge with information so the more I knew, the more I wanted to learn. They say when the student is ready the teacher shows up. Well chile, I was in the front seat of the class getting a lesson that would carry me for the rest of my days.

Different parts of my body would warm up sporadically for no rhyme or reason. It started with my earlobes. Sometimes my knee would warm up or my calf muscle would get hot out of the blue. My dreams became more vivid and lucid. I was having visions so often that I decided to make a dream journal to have something to reflect back on. Not knowing that most of these dreams would eventually come true. While I was having hot flashes on my body, Kory was having cold flashes in his. I remember being at home one Saturday morning and he ran into my room hysterical.

"Mom! Mom! I feel a cold feeling." He yelled

"Okay then put a shirt on."

"No mom I feel a cold feeling. Like something is walking through me!"

I was warm, but I could tell by the look in his eyes that he wasn't making this up. So, I walked over to him as he stood in the middle of the room shaking. From where I was standing it was warm. The closer I got to him, the colder it got. It was almost as if he was standing inside a freezer. All around his body I could feel a cool breeze. It was cold like winter time kinda cold. He wasn't making this up. I knew I had to calm him down before he lost his mind. I told him it was just his angels protecting him. It was the only thing I knew to say in order to take away his fear. I had no idea what he was experiencing but I knew he was special so I believed him.

The same night, I had a dream that there were people walking around my house. They were on the stairwell, in the hallway, in my kitchen; everywhere! They were walking around like zombies except they looked like regular people. I was yelling at them saying, "who are you?" No response. No one would look at me. They were walking around my house as if I wasn't there. Finally, I saw a man with black hair and piercing ocean blue eyes. He smiled at me and I relaxed. Then a lady passed by me in the hallway and I asked, "why won't you speak to me? Who are you!" She stopped dead in her tracks, looked at me and said, "we can't tell you who we are because you're not the only one who can see us." In the dream I was looking for Kory. I looked out the window and he was sitting in the middle of the backyard playing with a toy. He was surrounded by people but he wasn't afraid, he was actually talking to them. I woke up.

God showed me that Kory could see the same things that I could, and that we were surrounded by angels. If there was ever a time where I felt alone, he constantly reassured me that he has sent angels to comfort and protect us. We are surrounded by angels, spirit guides and guardian angels. Psalms 91:11 For he shall give his angels charge over thee, to keep thee in all thy ways.

Even though my speaking engagements seemed to dry up, I was still seeking out opportunities for my other gifts. I am a model, poet and author. I was blessed to be featured in *Essence* Magazine's first natural hair edition, with Kerry Washington on the cover. I've done some runway modeling even though I'm only 5'3 but I didn't have an agent, publicist or manager to help me.

One day I decided to search for a talent agent in the Oklahoma City area, in hopes to get my modeling career off the ground. Mind you, we are talking about Oklahoma, so there wasn't much opportunity to blow up anyway. I knew that I could only get so far there but it was worth a try. I was determined to be successful. By this time, I had written 4 books and produced a spoken word Cd. I had enough material to show an agent that I was serious about my career, and I had gotten this far with no help at all.

I ran across a lady named Mary Ann Morgan. She had an out of state phone number, but her business address was in Oklahoma City. As a matter of fact, it was five minutes from my apartment! So, I emailed this lady and told her who I was, what I do and what I was looking for. She was the only person to respond.

"Can you come by the office tomorrow at 5pm?"
I was excited! Finally, someone responded to my request for an agent. This was big! I didn't know what to wear to the meeting. I wanted her to see me in my natural state and not go in there pretending to be someone that I wasn't. I didn't put on any makeup. I didn't wear a suit either. I was casual but cute. I pulled up to this building and the first thing I noticed was there was only one car in the parking lot. Remember I found this lady by searching for talent agents. I brought my books, a copy of Essence

magazine, photos and business cards with me. I was prepared! I walked into the office and there was nothing in there but one long table. It wasn't even a professional cherry wood table, it was a fold out table. The walls were an empty canvas. There was no carpet. There was no office desk or receptionist. Nothing. The lady didn't greet me at the door, she just yelled, "come on in."

I walked in and there she sat at this long white fold out table.

"Hi there," I said nervously.

"Come on in."

I went over to the table and she stood up and shook my hand. I laid my material down and sat down in the chair across from her.

"Please excuse my office. We just purchased this building, so we haven't set everything up yet."

"No problem."

"Let me give you a tour."

She stood up and walked me through the building.

"This will be my office. We are going to hang pictures of all the models on this wall. We will set up a short runway here for the models to practice their strut," she continued.

I followed her from one room to another, nodding my head and imagining the vision she had for the building. We walked back to the table and sat down.

"So what brings you here?" she asked.

"Well I'm looking for a talent agent."

"Tell me a little bit about yourself."

I told her who I was and what I did. I showed her the Essence magazine picture to give her a visual of how I look in print. I gave her a copy of each book and my CD.

"You've been working pretty hard I see."

"Yes ma'am."

"What vision do you have for yourself?"

"Well I will be on the cover of a magazine."

"And you will," she agreed. What else?

"I will be a bestselling author."

"And you will," she agreed. What else?"

"I will be on TV."

"And you will," she agreed. What else?

"I will be on a Covergirl commercial."

"Eh," she disagreed. What else?

By this time I'm like, what do you mean Eh. But I indulged.

"I will be on a billboard in New York."

"And you will," she replied.

I thought to myself okay this is getting weird.

"It's cold in here, isn't it?" she asked.

"Yes, it is a bit chilly."

She walked over to the thermostat to see if it was working and it was. The room was unreasonably cold. She sat back down across from me and smiled.

"Let me see your hand," she said.

I reached out my right hand. She turned it over and started looking at the lines on my palms.

"You will be very successful."

I'm thinking to myself, okay what the hell is going on. I didn't show it on my face, but I was weirded out at this point.

"Let me tell you who I am," she says.

"My name is Mary Ann Morgan. I am a psychic. Have you ever heard of me?"

"No ma'am."

"I have worked with the A&E channel to help find missing children. I have been on the todays show,

Discovery channel and the Larry King show to name a few."

"Oh wow."

"I knew you were coming today. I knew when you walked in that you would be somebody big."

The room seemed to get colder and colder by the minute. Out of nowhere, she claps her hands in the air and says," QUIET!" My eyes bucked.

"You have a lot of angels around you."

I'm still in shock not saying anything. I'm trying to figure out who she's telling to be quiet.

"They have a lot to say about you."

"What are they saying?"

"I can't tell you but its good."

"Okay," I replied with one eyebrow raised.

"Are you ready for everywhere you go, people will know who you are?"

"Well I'm pretty well known here in Okc."

"No, I mean like the paparazzi. A celebrity. Are you ready for everyone to know who you are? It's big, it's so big I can't even tell you."

I'm silent at his point.

"I know that you're a poet but I see you acting."

"I don't know how to act."

"I know that you like Oklahoma City but your gonna have to move."

"Nah I can't see myself living anywhere but here. I've made a name for myself here."

"Honey your going to be big. You have a lot of energy surrounding you. I knew from the minute you walked in this room that greatness is on you. It's so big I can't even tell you." She says with confidence.

Now I see why it was so cold in that room. I sat back in my chair shocked, dazed and confused. I googled a talent agent and ran up on a psychic. What in the world is going on? Funny thing is I believed her. I didn't know how, when or where this was going to happen, but deep down in my soul I believed this woman. She had no reason to lie to me. I didn't give her any money. She had nothing to gain by telling me this. She took copies of all my books, shook my hand and said, "I'll be in touch." I have never heard anything else from that woman.

I was too comfortable in Oklahoma City to even think about moving. I didn't know anything about acting and it was nowhere on my radar. Poetry and modeling was the only thing I saw for myself. I am not good with change. Once I get settled at a job I stay there. I like consistency and stability. This could be a good and bad trait, because on one hand being organized and structured has helped me this far. On the other hand, it prevented me from thinking outside of the box and trying new things. If I wasn't open minded enough to consider stepping out of my comfort zone, how could I accomplish all my dreams? Everything happens for a reason. I was supposed to get laid off. I was too comfortable. I was supposed to meet Mary Ann. I was guided to search for a talent agent at that time for a reason. My intuition led me to her. She gave me something to think about but moving was just out of the question for me.

The summer of 2014 was the beginning of my new life and the end of everything I knew as normal. I spent a great deal of time retraining my mind to only think and speak positive regardless of how I was feeling. Most people take pride in "telling it like it is" without realizing their role in the perpetual cycle they are creating for themselves. So, instead of telling it like it is, I started telling it how I wanted it to be. Romans 4:17 says to call those things that are not as though they were. That's exactly what I started to do.

Instead of making a vision board, I created a magical creation box. An idea I got from reading *Ask and it is Given* by Esther and Jerry Hicks. Its no different from a vision board, I just found it to be easier to manage. Habakkuk **2:2** says to write the vision and make it plain upon tables, that he may run that read it. I bought a cute cherry wood box and on top of the box I wrote "everything in this box already is." Next, I went through old magazines and cut out pictures, words and phrases that matched my goals. If I couldn't find a picture, then I just wrote it on a piece of paper and put it in my box. I wanted a new bicycle, so I found a nice ten-speed bike online, printed it off and put it in my box. I even put the amount I wanted to spend which was no more than $180. My list included things like a new vacuum, a black blazer jacket, a Jeep Wrangler, a credit score of 700, debt free signs, amazon best seller stickers etc. I even cut out a picture of Oprah sitting on her couch and glued a picture of myself sitting next to her. One day I will meet Oprah! Nothing is too big or small to go inside that box. If you're going to dream you might as well dream big.

From my studies on the law of attraction I knew that whatever I focused my attention on is what I would attract. It didn't stop with my thoughts either. I knew that whatever I said, I would get. I knew that whatever I wrote down, I would receive as well. So not only did I think about the things I wanted, I started saying it out loud. I would make lists of goals, read them out loud then put them in my magical creation box. I wrote down states I wanted to perform in like California, New York and Atlanta. I wrote the stages I wanted to perform on like Apache Café and Nuyorican Poet café to name a few.

I created a list of affirmations and read them out loud twice a day. To this day, I have this list memorized and say it out loud every morning. If there was a time when I was having a not so good day, I would say those affirmations to raise my vibration. If we stay in a state of gratitude, we can attract the things we want into our lives. If we are in a state of complaining or having pity parties, we repel the things we want and start attracting unwanted people, situations and things into our existence.

Not only is it important to write it down and speak it, it is imperative that we visualize it as well. I took full advantage of not having a job. Every morning I would sip my coffee, and lay down on my couch with my eyes closed and visualize how I wanted my life to be. I was very detailed with my imagination. I saw myself speaking on stages with sold out seats. I could hear the crowd responding to my poems. I could feel the crowd's energy cheering me on. I saw myself sitting in that brand-new Jeep Wrangler. I visualized all my bills being paid on time. I saw my credit score going up. I saw checks coming in the mail. I saw myself sitting with Oprah, sipping tea and talking about how I made it on her show. I saw it, smelled it, and felt it as if it already happened.

Our brain does not know the difference between a visualization and reality. So, when we hold a thought for more than 16 seconds, our brain stores it in our memory bank as something that has already happened. The more you think about it, the easier it is to attract it into your existence because you have created a match to the thing you desire. Once you create a vibrational match for it, your body starts sending out a frequency into the universe saying, "I want this." Your job is just to wait for it.

Consistency is the key to anything. Whatever you do for 21 days becomes a habit. When something is a habit, you do it without consciously thinking about it. The goal is to think, say and speak on a thing for at least 21 days so it will become second nature for you. Faith without works is dead. Whatever your little heart's desire is, first you must believe it is possible to attain it. Your work is to ask, seek and knock. We have not because we ask not. Some of us don't ask because we don't believe we can attain it. When we don't believe, we don't ask and when we don't ask we don't get!

Now here comes the fun part! The first thing I manifested was my bicycle. I had a clear vision of the kind of bike I wanted, and I knew that I didn't want to pay more than $180 for it. I went to Walmart and saw the exact same bike I wanted but the bike was $300. No Bueno. Something told me to go to Academy sports and guess what? The bike was there on sale for $150! I bought the bike and a bike rack. Some guy put the bike rack on the back of my Camaro in the parking lot for me. I was so excited I went to Lake Hefner and rode 10 miles non- stop.

Once your faith is rewarded, it becomes more exciting to manifest your desires. When you see that its working, it's easier to stay focused on the positives and watch what you say. Start off small and work your way up to the big things so you don't get discouraged. I mean let's face it, we all want a million dollars right? Even though it is attainable, a more realistic goal you could start off with is $100. Write a check out to yourself for $100 and put it in your magical creation box.

Too many times we stop doing a thing because we don't see any results. We go to the gym for three days, and if we don't see that six-pack coming in, we stop going. Timing is everything. The money that your waiting on is attached to a person who must be intuitive enough to sow into you. The job that your waiting on may be attached to someone else passing or retiring. You never know what the holdup is for the thing you're believing for. Once you set your mind on something long enough, your body will send out a request to the universe to send that thing to you! The universe will conspire to give you everything you ask for. That's why you must keep your faith, be consistent and believe that it will come to pass. Don't quit! You are more powerful than you know.

Meditating increased my intuition, so I started paying attention to everything. Signs, symbols and synchronicity became my guide. I also had to be mindful of the people I surrounded myself with. We know that everybody doesn't believe as we do. Everybody is not conscious of speaking sickness and poverty over themselves. Some people aren't aware of the power of words and it made me distance myself from the crowd. I realize we can't control what other people say or do but, we do have a choice in whether to participate in it. I chose not to. I became a hermit. When people spoke doubt, fear, lack and sickness in conversations, it made me cringe. They know not what they do, but I didn't want no parts of it.

I avoided negative people at all cost. I mean let's be honest. I didn't have a job. I didn't know what the future holds for me. I was trying to manifest some stuff. The last thing I needed was someone else's negative energy and drama interfering with my progress! People said I changed. I wasn't fun anymore. I didn't partake in certain conversations because I was serious about growing. When life knocks you down, you must look inwardly and do the soul work necessary for you to grow. Yea, it's cute to have a new outfit and the latest shoes and purses. But what does your soul look like? How do you treat people? What kind of attitude do you have towards people who appear to be doing better than you? What could you possibly change about yourself? Do you even like you? Ask yourself the hard questions. You must do the soul work. Because where God is trying to take you, he won't allow you to remain the same. You can't be ugly on the inside and all dressed up on the outside with negative energy. Your toxic spirit will destroy everything you worked so hard for. Do the soul work at all cost. People who win the lottery and go broke in 3 years lose the money because they were spiritually broke to begin with. A poverty mentality will deplete anything that looks like abundance. That's why you see people with couches on the front porch. Cars parked in the grass. Refrigerators in the front yard, in a nice neighborhood. Whatever is in you is bound to come out and show up on the outside. I knew that the only way I could keep my vibration up was to distance myself from certain people and that's exactly what I did. They will get over it. The people who stand by you in the long run, will either grow with you or go without you. Learn how to leave the baggage at the door.

The more soul work you do, the more intuitive you will be. Its like a detox. Once you get all the junk out of the way, the pureness of who were at birth will shine through. Your aura will be brighter. Your skin will be healthier. You will stick out like a sore thumb. Everything about you will speak of a higher vibration. You will be guided by spirit. You will be more in tune with your environment and nature. You will start to pay attention to the subtle nudges that God is holding your hand every step of the way. Everything will feel, taste and look better. Your life will be delicious and exciting!

By this time, God had my undivided attention. I remember waking up early to go grocery shopping with Kory. The morning started out as a normal day. (as normal as it could be in my house) Kory was taking his time getting ready and I was rushing him, so we could hurry up and get back and relax for the rest of the day. He was moving at a snail's pace and I was agitated to say the least. We finally made it to the car but before I could start the car, I felt a warm presence on the right side of my face. I thought hmm, ok that was weird. I knew it was spirit. It was a comforting warmth that you couldn't ignore. I put the car in reverse and proceeded towards 122nd street.

I merged onto the Broadway Extension exit and that's when it got real. I was driving in the middle lane of the three-lane highway, going about 55mph. The cars in front of me were cruising right along and everything was peaceful. For some reason I decided to get in the far-right lane. I put my blinker on and merged over with no problem. In a split second I heard "BOOM!" the sound of medal crashing. I looked to my left, and this man driving a pickup truck, two lanes over, was out of control! He crashed into the car in front of him and then his truck turned sideways on two wheels! By now he is driving parallel across two lanes headed straight for my car. When he crossed over to the lane next to me, the car that was in that lane hit him and then he spun out of control in the middle of the highway. I looked in my rearview mirror and there were about 6 cars involved in that accident. It felt almost as if time stopped. I was in a bubble so to speak. I could see him coming in my direction but not one time was I afraid. I didn't speed up, I didn't slow down. I didn't swerve or try to avoid the accident. I didn't even feel like I had control of my car! I was stuck in a time warp. Everything was moving in slow motion. Had I not switched lanes when I did, he would have hit the side of my door, at a high rate of speed, and I would have been involved in that 6-car pileup.

Kory was crying, and I was shaken up just looking in my rearview mirror. The devastation behind me was indescribable. That could have easily been me. I broke out in tears on my way to the store. I couldn't help but praise God! The warmth that I felt before we got on that highway was the presence of an angel. Once again, I felt a tangible expression of Gods unconditional love saying, "I got you."

We made it to the grocery store in one piece. After paying for the stuff, I held onto the receipt, so I could deduct the amount I spent from my checking account. I had an app on my phone to keep up with my daily transactions. I would make sure the amount on the app matched the amount on my banking app. I pulled up the banking app while we were in the car and there was a charge of $407 from Sams. I didn't shop online at Sams nor did I own a Sams card. It appears the charge was made a few days ago but since I hadn't spent any money, I hadn't checked my balance on my banking app. Something was clearly wrong, and I was going to get to the bottom of it as soon as I got home.

As we were carrying the groceries to our apartment, I noticed a long box on my porch. I know I didn't order anything, but I took it the house to see what it was. It was a Dyson vacuum! It said it came from Sams.com so I called the customer service number. I told the lady I didn't order a vacuum and that they charged my card $407. She asked for the serial number on the back of the vacuum, so I gave it to her.

"Ma'am I'm not pulling up any online orders for that serial number."

"Well I didn't order this vacuum so ya'll need to come pick it up."

"There is no record of that vacuum in our system."

Mind you, I called the number on the piece of paper that came in the package. So, I had to call my bank and tell them I have been wrongfully charged for something I did not order. I'm cheap so if I was going to buy a vacuum I sure as hell wouldn't buy one for $407. The bank canceled my debit card and sent me another one. She said I would receive a refund in 3 business days. How could someone order a vacuum with my debit card, and have it sent to my house without there being any record of the order online? For one week I left that vacuum in the box, waiting for someone to pick it up. Nobody came. I must have been a vacuuming machine. A $407 vacuum! I used the heck out of that thing. Remember my magical creation box? I wrote down that I wanted a vacuum. I know God answers prayers, but I was thinking more along the lines of something $40. Ask and it is given.

One of my favorite things to do is thrift shopping. I love going to goodwill and finding sales. One day I went to the goodwill store in Edmond, and the first thing I saw was a black Calvin Klein blazer jacket. You would have thought I won the lottery! It's like it was waiting for me. It was the perfect size too. This was the jacket I've been wanting. Not only was it just $4 but it was brand new. Remember that magical creation box? Inside of it was a picture of a black blazer jacket. Ask and it is given.

Kory had been pestering me about a dog. I wasn't really a pet person, nor did I know how to care for a dog. He begged and begged until I gave in. I googled dogs in the Oklahoma City area, and ran across the humane societies website. After searching through the website, I ran across a cute dog with a red bandana tied around his neck. I thought to myself, that's the one! I didn't show the dog to Kory because I didn't want to get his hopes up. I also wanted to see if he would pick out the same dog that I saw online. I took Kory to the dog shelter and we walked up and down the isles looking at the dogs. There had to be at least 100 dogs in that place. It was loud and cold. The dogs were barking and jumping up on the fences. They had everything from puppies to pit bulls. Some were big, and some were small. We walked up and down every isle, but Kory didn't seem to be impressed with anything so far. We turned the corner and there was the dog that I saw online. He looked so sad, huddled up in the corner all by himself. I didn't say anything to Kory. We walked past the dog and he looked back and said, "that's the one mom."

He picked the same dog that I picked without even knowing it. We named him King.

King was a nice addition to our family. I must admit, the dog got on my nerves following me from one room to the next, but I really did enjoy his company. One day as I was sitting on the couch, King jumped on the couch and laid down on my legs. He turned around and looked me dead in the eyes. For a moment I could feel my granny's presence. I know this sounds crazy but I'm not kidding. My granny was a dog lover. She had 3 dogs before she passed away. She talked to those dogs like they were her kids. I have never been an animal person, but this dog pulled on my heart strings. He stared at me for what felt like an eternity and I instantly started crying. I texted a friend of mine and told her that I could feel granny's presence in the dog. King jumped off the couch and went back into Kory's room to lay down on his bunk bed with him. A few minutes later, Kory came into the living room and said, "Mom you know what's weird? He asked.

"What?"

"King acts like granny."

That was his little minds interpretation of feeling granny's presence. I almost pissed my pants. How did this boy know what I was feeling? I just texted my friend saying this very thing just a moment ago. I shook my head. This boy ain't gone worry me.

Intuitive Guidance

The more in tune we are with our higher selves, the better we can recognize when our angels are trying to get our attention. Angels speak to you in many ways and one of them is by code. Everyone senses spirit differently. Once you figure out which of your seven-senses resonates with you, then you will be able to recognize when angels are trying to give you a message. You also must slow down enough, be present enough, and learn how to go with the flow enough, so you won't miss it. It's hard enough trying to get someone to put their phone down, let alone be present. You must learn how to be where you're at.

The seven senses are clairvoyance (clear vision) clairaudience (clear hearing), clairsentience (clear feeling), clairscent (clear smelling), clairtangency (clear touching), clairgustance (clear tasting) and clairempathy (clear emotion). I've always sensed spirit with my feelings, vision and hearing. You may sense spirit by smelling cigarette smoke after a loved one has passed. You may be able to taste a substance without putting it in your mouth. Maybe you hear a voice in your inner ear or get goose bumps out of nowhere. Whatever the case, we all can communicate with our angels. They will use numbers, feathers, animals, nature, music and people to get our attention.

With my heightened awareness to the spiritual realm, and the presence of angels protecting me, I started to notice numbers. I remember like it was yesterday. I was sitting in church, and I looked down at my watch and it was **12:22**. I didn't think anything of it because at this time I wasn't into numbers. After church was over, I hung around for a bit to mingle with some friends. I looked at my watch again and this time it was 1:**22**. Hmm, that's odd, I thought to myself. From that day forward, I started seeing the number **22** everywhere! It was on billboards, license plates, signs, phone numbers, receipts, everywhere! I would even hear it in songs or commercials on the radio. It was brought to my attention so much that I decided to google it.

I know you've been wondering this whole time, what is the meaning of **22**? As you can see from the beginning of this book, up until this point, the number **22** had been a part of my entire life. I had no idea until now that this number has been guiding me. How would I know this had it not gotten my attention? This is proof that the laws of the universe are working whether you are consciously aware of it. I was never into numbers. I've never done any research on the meaning of numbers. They surely don't teach you that in church. The only number I knew was 10% and that was to pay my tithes.

Angel number **22** possesses the energies of your biggest dreams and deepest desires. If you keep seeing **22**, it's because you are finally on your way to manifesting them. Angel Number **22** means power and purpose. This number might be communicating that this is the ideal time for you to pursue your dreams. Angel Number **22** can empower you to accomplish these dreams and transform them into your reality. It also signifies balance and harmony. Things that have been affecting your life's balance and creating discord will finally be gone. Angel

Number **22** is **a message from your angels** to maintain your convictions and keep an optimistic outlook and a **positive attitude** as your desires are currently being manifested for you.

I don't find it a coincidence that I didn't start seeing this number, until I was laid off. I was at a point in my life where I had nothing else to lose. Even though I didn't notice this number until 2014, the power of **22** has carried me my entire life. Everything is purposed. Remember, my daddy was **22** years old when he had me. God is the author and the finisher of our faith. We come into this world with a purpose that was ordained by God before the foundation of this world. Everything has meaning. Numerology, astrology, anatomy, angels, spirit guides, master teachers (depending on your religious beliefs) and nature. All things are working together for your good!

Working at that job for 12 years was affecting my life's balance and creating discord. It interfered with the goals I set for myself. It was time to go! Everything I'd been through in my past relationships was creating discord. It was time to go! (you need to read my autobiography *Thick Skin* to understand my excitement). The negative people I separated myself from had to go! They were creating discord! Discord means disharmony. When you are in disharmony, you are operating in a lower vibrational frequency. When you are operating in a lower vibrational frequency, you can't attract the things you want! Your spirit will repel the very things you are asking for, because you are not in vibrational alignment with it. The soul work I was doing was setting me up for a life that I could only dream of.

Right now, you may be reflecting on numbers that keep popping up in your life. Your number may not be 22. It could be 333, 11, 555, 363 or any number sequence for that matter. The point is, whenever you start to notice the same number sequence popping up, take note. Look it up. Your angels are trying to convey a message to you. Different number sequences will pop up at different points in your life. Depending on your needs at the time, angels will try to give you guidance, by showing you a number. Your job is to pay attention.

Around January of 2015 my unemployment benefits were running out. I still hadn't touched my 401k money, but I knew something had to give soon. My speaking engagements were dried up. I might have had one event per month if that. I was still adding things to my magical creation box. I was still writing out checks to myself and visualizing money coming to me. I was still saying my daily affirmations and speaking things into existence. I had a few break downs where I would sit on my patio and just cry. Not knowing what the future holds, or what I was supposed to be doing was nerve wracking. I knew that I would be successful one day, but I had no idea how or when it would happen. If ever there was a time where I doubted God, I would see the number **22**.

On May 18th, 2015, I picked Kory up from school. We stopped by Grandy's to get our favorite chicken fried steak meal to go. On the way home, Kory looked at me and said, "mom I think we should move."

"What? No. Why?"

"I don't know."

"Where would we move to Kory?"

"To a big city, like California or Atlanta."

"Nah we can't move. I like Oklahoma City."

"But mom its time for us to move."

"We'll see Kory," I dismissed him. You would think by now I would stop dismissing my son. Obviously, I didn't learn my lesson the first time. The next morning as Kory was asleep, I got up to make a cup of coffee. The morning was like any other morning. I sat in the living room with the tv off, enjoying my coffee in peace and quiet. I figured since he was sound asleep, now would be the perfect time for me to meditate. I sat in the chair in an upright position and quieted my soul.

After about 15 minutes, I opened my eyes, exhaled and sat there for a second. I walked into the kitchen to make me another cup of coffee, and I heard a voice that sounded like it came out of the walls.

"MOVE TO ATLANTA"

I stood frozen in the middle of the kitchen, looking around to see where that voice came from. This voice wasn't like the baby's voice I heard when my daddy passed. This voice was loud like the lion's voice in my dream. It came from inside my inner ear, but it felt like it came out of the walls. I peeked into Kory's bedroom and he was sound asleep. I walked all through that apartment thinking I was hearing things. I heard it again.

"MOVE TO ATLANTA"

By this time I'm freaking out. I started talking to myself. I'm like "nah I can't move to Atlanta. I don't know anybody in Atlanta. I don't have money to move to Atlanta." I was tripping. I called my friend and said, "I know this is going to sound crazy, but God just told me to move to Atlanta."

"Then you better go."

"What? No. Why? How?"

49

"Girl if God told you to go you better go!"
I still wasn't convinced I was supposed to go. Even though this was the 3rd time I heard it! (hard headed) Remember the psychic told me I was going to have to move. Then Kory, now God himself spoke. I still wasn't having it. For two nights it was on my mind heavy. I didn't sleep a wink. I thought something was wrong with me because I couldn't fall asleep. I was walking around like a zombie. My heart was beating fast, I didn't know if I was coming or going. It was on my mind so heavy, I couldn't watch tv for 2 days! God would not let me rest until I surrendered to his will. Just like the story in Genesis **32:26** Like Jacob, I was wrestling with God. We know God always wins.

That same night, Kory wanted to sleep in the bed with me. As we were laying there preparing to fall asleep, he says, "mom, somebody is in the room with us."
"Where?"
He pointed to the left-hand corner of the room.
"There."
I couldn't see anything or feel anything, but I knew he was telling the truth.
"It's okay Pooda. It's just your angels watching over you."
"Okay."
He turned over and just like that he was sound asleep. When I finally managed to doze off, I felt a pressure on my back. I was having an out of body experience. I could see myself asleep, but I was in that scary paralyzed state where I couldn't move. A man stood at the foot of my bed. I asked him who he was, and he told me his name was James. He had ocean blue eyes just like the other angels in my dreams. He had a very friendly face. I asked if he was my guardian angel and he said yes. I hugged him tight.

50

He didn't give me a message or anything. He just stood there. I woke up.

I believe God had to send my guardian angel to visit me because I was so afraid to move. I don't like change. I didn't know anybody in Atlanta except for one person, whom I hadn't spoken to in over 10 years. I was running out of money. I didn't know what he was telling me to go to Atlanta for, but I knew I had to trust him. I finally surrendered.

The next morning, I reached out to that old friend to see if it would be okay for us to stay with her. If I was going to move to Atlanta, first I needed to feel it out. The last time we'd spoken, she was living in Baltimore, Md. I don't find it a coincidence that now she is living in Atlanta. She told me that she lived in Stone Mountain, Ga, and that me and Kory could stay with her for as long as we needed. She told me about some apartments close by her house that were nice. She gave me the name of the schools nearby and left it up to me to do the research.

I spent the entire day researching the cost of living, different counties, crime statistics and school districts. I've lived in Oklahoma my entire life. There is no traffic. There are seven counties in Oklahoma City to choose from. It's not hard to decide what school district you want to live in. Oklahoma is simple. Georgia has 159 counties! How in the world was I supposed to know where to go once I got there? Since the only city I knew about was Stone Mountain, I decided to start researching that area first. I looked at the crime statistics surrounding that apartment complex that she mentioned, and compared that to the school ranking. It was bad. There was no diversity. It was

95% black and 5% other. I love my people, but I didn't want to live where there was no diversity. Kory wasn't used to that. He had Mexican, white and black friends so I had to make the best decision for him. I researched some other apartments in the Stone Mountain area that were nice, but again, I wasn't impressed with the school system. At one point I got frustrated, and was about to settle on this one school, but God put a stop to that immediately.

I logged onto Facebook, and this news story kept rolling down my timeline. The headline read, "Teacher arrested after claims he let students have sex in storage closet." I have no idea why Atlanta news was on my feed because I lived in Oklahoma. The same story kept popping up all day long. Something told me (my intuition) to click on the article, and low and behold, it was the assigned school for that apartment complex! My eyes bucked. My mouth dropped. I was in shock. Every time I tried to make a decision, my angels would stop me in my tracks. God would not let me fail. Talk about divine intervention.

That night I packed one gym bag for myself and one for Kory. We had enough clothes to last us seven days. Friday, May 22nd was the last day of school. Since the kids only had to go for a half a day, I decided to head to Atlanta around 1pm. We took highway 40E from Oklahoma City to Arkansas. Then highway 22 from Memphis to Birmingham. Highway 20E took us straight to Atlanta. It took us 12 hours to get to Stone mountain Georgia. I had no idea what I was going to do once I got there. I just wanted to see how it felt and if Kory would like it too. My friend set up her guest room to accommodate us. They made us feel right at home.

The next morning, I logged onto Facebook and saw a flier from one of my followers in Atlanta. It was for an open mic poetry night, on Sunday at the Dream Café. Something told me to inbox the guy to let him know I was in town.

"Hey I'm in Atlanta, are you still having your poetry night?" I asked.

"Yes ma'am and you'll be a surprise guest."

And just like that, a door was opened. I had a whole day to prepare. We spent the entire Saturday checking out the list of apartments I had written down. It took us 45 minutes to an hour to get from one place to another. On some highways there was a many as 8 lanes! In Oklahoma it only takes about 15-20 to get anywhere! The traffic alone was enough to make you throw in the towel.

We went to Cobb county and checked out apartments in Marietta and Smyrna. Smyrna was nice, but expensive. My apartment in Oklahoma City was only $700 a month. I needed to find something in that same price range. The apartments in Smyrna were so nice, I almost didn't feel worthy to walk on the grounds. The landscaping was immaculate. The streets were wide and paved in dark black cement, like they were brand new. There wasn't a pot hole in sight. Almost every car in the parking lot was a luxury vehicle. They had Olympic sized swimming pools with gated communities. This was certainly not something I was used to. The rent for a two-bedroom apartment started at $955. No Bueno.

The very last apartment I checked out, had the split floor plan that I wanted. It came equipped with a washer and drier, vaulted ceilings and a huge patio. The cost was $1200 for 2 bedrooms. By this time, I'm aggravated. Wondering why God would send me to

Atlanta, knowing good and well I couldn't afford to live there. I didn't have a job. I didn't know anything about the schools or where to live except for what I read online. I was literally walking by faith.

I stood in the parking lot of those luxury apartments and pointed directly at them. I said, "I don't want to pay $1200 for an apartment.

God please direct me to an apartment that looks just like these, in my price range."

The apartments that were too cheap, had the worst school districts and the highest crime. The most expensive apartments had the highest-ranking schools. By the end of the day, I had about 20 brochures in hand and a defeated spirit. We drove back to Stone Mountain and relaxed for the rest of the night.

The next morning, something told me to check out Lithia Springs. I remember someone on Facebook mentioning that area to me, but somehow, I forgot. Kory and I, woke up early Sunday morning, and drove from Stone Mountain to Lithia springs, in all that traffic. It took us 45 minutes to get there. The first place we walked into was really nice. It was a gated community with the same amenities. The price was $920. I walked into the office and the lady asked me what I was looking for. I told her that I needed a two-bedroom apartment.

"What brings you to Atlanta?

"I'm an artist and I'm moving down here for the opportunities."

"Oh really? What kind of artist are you?"

"I'm a poet, author and model."

"Really. I would love to hear a poem."

"Oh no ma'am. My poetry is not roses are red violets are blue kind of poetry."

"So you speak that real stuff huh."

"Yes ma'am."

"Just give me a sample please."

"Okay, you asked for it."

I stood in the middle of the office and performed one my best pieces. I looked over at the lady, and she was in tears. Half way through my poem, the other lady who had her back towards me, had turned around. Her mouth dropped. She was in tears. When I finished speaking, they both stood up and gave me a hug.

"You're in the right place."

"Yes ma'am."

"There is so much opportunity for you here. You will be very successful."

"Thank you."

I walked out of that office feeling more confident than before. There were only two apartments on my list and that was one of them. We arrived at the next one and I instantly didn't like the outside. They looked older than the others, but they were doing some construction, so we checked them out anyway. We walked into the office and the man behind the desk was talking on his cell phone. I stood at the door and he summoned for me to sit down. We sat down for about five minutes before he finally got off the phone.

"What can I do for you?" he asked.

"I'm looking for a two-bedroom apartment."

"Here's our floorplans and prices." He hands me the brochures. As I'm looking over the brochure, some resident walks into the office and interrupts our meeting.

"I just wanna know why ya'll haven't fixed the leak in my apartment yet."

"Sir, I'm with a customer right now. Can you come back a little later?"

The resident storms out, cursing under his breath.

"I'm sorry about that. Are you ready to go look?"

Before I could respond, another resident walked in upset.

"Why ya'll keep losing my proof of insurance? This is the 3rd time I've had to bring this paper to ya'll!"

"Sir, I'm with a customer. Can you come back a little later?" The office manager responds with an attitude.

At this point I'm thinking this complex is a no go. They had too much mess going on and I haven't even seen the apartment yet. I took the piece of paper the guy gave me and wrote on the back of it. "Don't move here. They don't fix nothing." I folded the paper and put it in my pocket. The man storms out of the office just like the last one did.

"I apologize. Would you mind following me in your car to the building?"

"Sure no problem."

Even though my mind was already made up, I didn't want to waste the time I'd already spent, so we viewed it anyway. When we got in the car, Kory says, "mom I don't think we should move here."

"Why Pooda?"

"Because they don't fix nothing."

I just shook my head. The prophet had spoken.

We pulled out of the complex and decided to head back to Stone Mountain before the three o'clock traffic hit. As we were driving down Thornton Road, I happened to see another complex on my right side. The sign read Crestmark apartments. We swerved into the complex so fast you would have thought the police were chasing us. The grounds were clean and tidy. They had the big patio that I liked. The swimming pool area was nice, and it was quiet. I walked into the office and the apartment manager was sweet and professional. The lady greeted us in a joyful manor. I had a good feeling about this place.

"What can I help you with today?"

"I'm interested in your two-bedroom units."

"Awesome! Here's our floorplans and pricing." She said excited.

I like this place already. She gave me a tour of the grounds and the two-bedroom unit. It was exactly like the apartment in Smyrna. It had the vaulted ceilings, separate laundry room, split floor plan and the huge patio. The rent was $860. When she told me the amount, I looked at Kory and we both smiled. I knew this was the right place. I didn't find out until later the zip code was 30122. I swear I can't make this stuff up! During our ride back to Stone Mountain, Kory says, "mom this place feels like home."

"You mean Georgia?"

"Yea it feels good."

"It does huh. I love the trees."

"Me too mom."

We didn't talk for the rest of the ride back. There was a peaceful, reassuring energy that echoed in the silence of the car. I knew this was the right place. I knew Georgia was where we needed to be. I didn't know how or when it was going to happen, but I no longer had doubts about it. Later on that night, we headed out to The Dream Café for the open mic. As soon as I walked in, the guy who ran the spot came over to me smiling. He recognized me from Facebook. He embraced me and offered me a bottle of water. He was so happy to see me. We sat down in the audience and waited for the show to begin.

"We have a special guest tonight. She came all the way from Oklahoma City. Ms. Kendal S. Turner ya'll!"

The audience cheered me on as I made my way to the stage. The guy told me to do three poems and that's exactly what I did. By the time I finished my last poem, everyone in the audience was crying, laughing, cheering and yelling. I got a standing ovation. It was an amazing experience. To close out the show, a young lady who owned the place performed. The first line of her poem read, "It's been **22** days since we've seen each other." I didn't hear anything else. My eyes got so big. Kory and I looked at each other and he said, "Mom she said **22**!" It was the craziest experience ever. One again God reassured me, I GOT YOU.

The next day, I felt an urgency in my spirit to go online and sign a lease at Crestmark. Without thinking, I logged onto their website, signed a lease and received my approval within minutes. They approved me for an apartment, without asking me for proof of income or anything! Look at God! The apartment number they gave me was 945 so I googled it.

Angel Number 945 is **a message from your angels** that you have been receiving intuitive and **angelic guidance** about your **life purpose** and **soul mission**. The guidance you have been receiving through your intuitive feelings, visions and **dreams** are connected to your **life purpose**, and your **angels** ask that you trust these messages and take positive action. You may need to make some much needed changes in your life and work diligently towards achieving your goals and aspirations. You may feel prompted to be of service to others and humanity as a whole. Trust that you have all the skills and talents you need to fulfill your **light working** mission.

The last three days in Atlanta, we decided to do some sightseeing. We went to the World of Coca-Cola museum and the Georgia Aquarium. We ate some good soul food, and I got to perform at Urban Grind on Thursday night. There was so much talent and opportunities in Atlanta that I didn't want to go back home. The people there were so progressive and helpful. They were friendly and didn't have that crab in a barrel mentality that I grew up experiencing. There was so much culture and diversity. The possibilities were endless. Now I understand why God told me to move. Now I understand why my engagements dried up in Oklahoma. There was nothing left for me to do there. The name that I made for myself would set the foundation for what God had in store for me. All I had to do was be obedient and follow my intuition.

When you listen to your intuition, you can't go wrong. Your spirit knows exactly what you need. We are pre-programed with our very own GPS system. As I stated in the beginning of the book, we are not taught to listen to ourselves. We are not taught to trust our intuition. Most of us have been bound by religion and traditions that have stripped us of our common sense. We must stop putting God in a box. He cannot be defined. He is bigger than our carnal minds can even fathom. He is omnipotent. He is omnipresent. He is the divine source of everything we see, feel, smell, touch and hear. I believe God is always speaking to us. His language is multidimensional. If the only way you seek to hear from God is through a pastor, you are limiting the divine wisdom that is available to all of us. All you have to do it tap in. You are a powerful soul.

You are pure to your core. You came from the source of all things which is unconditional love! You have the power to move mountains. You have the power to lay hands on the sick and perform miracles. You are not a label. You are not your divorce. You are not your struggle. You are not defined by your parenting abilities or the number of degrees you have. You are so much more than that. It took me 38 years to figure this out.

The drive back to Oklahoma City was miserable. Neither one of us wanted to go back but we had to prepare to move. I signed a year lease at an apartment complex with no job. I was set to move in on 7-25-15. I took out my 401k and put the rest in God's hands. My oldest son, Courtland was headed off to college. He decided to stay in Oklahoma City, to be closer to family. My last weekend in Oklahoma City, my friends threw me a going away party, and we danced the night away. It was an emotional day for them, but I was so anxious to move, that I couldn't even cry.

We settled into our new place nicely. Kory adjusted very easily. He is a kid magnet, so he had no problem making new friends. I hit the ground running. I performed at every open mic event, with business cards on hand. The first time I performed at Apache Café, was for an Apollo style open mic competition. Out of 17 artists, I came in 5th place. Remember that magical creation box? Apache Café was on the list! I let my intuition guide me and I was always at the right place at the right time.

Not even three months of living in Atlanta, a big opportunity fell in my lap. I was scrolling down my Facebook feed, when I saw a post from a guy looking for models. I wasn't sure if he was looking for runway type of models or fashion models. I'm only 5'3, so at first I hesitated in sending him a message. Something told me to message him anyway.

"Hello, I saw your post about models. Are you looking for runway models or fashion models?" I asked.

"Fashion models."

"So you don't have to be tall?"

"No ma'am. Can you get here in one hour?"

"Yes!"

"Wear all black."

He sent me the address and I was out the door in a matter of minutes. I had no idea what this photoshoot was for. I didn't know what the location was. The only thing I knew was the time and place. I ended up in midtown Atlanta. The name of the shop was The Purple Door salon. I walked in and sat down next to the other models. The ladies were very feminine with high heels on. I walked in there with a blazer jacket, v- neck t -shirt and slacks. I was comfortable in all of my swag. As I waited in my seat, I turned around and low and behold. The phone number painted on the outside of the window was 404-222-9553. I can't make this stuff up!

Finally, a lady came over to me and asked me to come with her. They could tell that I wasn't a girly girl, so they wanted to dress me in something I would be comfortable wearing. They gave me a black leather jacket with zippers on it and some black skinny jeans. There was a very handsome guy who had dreadlocks like mine, so they paired us together, and told us we would be a couple. After my makeup was done, I waited another hour before it was our turn to shoot. Out of nowhere, Dwight Eubanks walks into the salon. Come to find out, he was the owner. A freaking celebrity! I was trying to keep my cool and not act star struck but my heart was racing. He walked in and had everybody's undivided attention. He looked at every model and critiqued them.

"Who did her hair?" He pointed at another girl.

"Do it over." He said.

Then he walked over to another girl.

"Who did her makeup? I don't like it."

Then he walked over to me.

"Oh you are beautiful." He smiled.

"Thank you."

"I love your hair."

"Thank you."

He sat down under a hair drier and started eating some chicken. They made some changes to my jewelry, so I ended up sitting next to him under another drier. I wanted to speak to him so bad, but I didn't know what to say. I figured I didn't have nothing to lose so I went for it.

"Do you mind if I can get a picture with you?" I asked.

"Sure!"

I leaned over and snapped three photos of us. He looked at them and said, "girl we cute." I smiled.

"What are you doing next week?" He asked.

"Nothing what's up?"

"You should come to my liquor launch party."

"Okay I will."

I was cool, calm and collected after that. I posted our pictures on Facebook and everybody was happy for my experience.

Although I was popular in Oklahoma City, I realized Atlanta did not know who I was. I had to start from the ground up and make a name for myself all over again. There were times when I would drive an hour to get to an event, just to perform one poem. I wasn't getting any features yet, so I wasn't getting paid. I went to open mics on Wednesday, Thursday, Friday, Saturday and Sunday. I was going broke on just gas money alone. I didn't give up though. The more I performed, the more my name started buzzing around the city. Eventually, all the big-time poets knew who I was.

One day one of my Facebook friends invited me to come speak at a church function. I hadn't performed at a church since my days in Oklahoma City. I was kind of over the church crowd, but I indulged anyway. I showed up early and met the guy for the first time. He was really impressed with me and told me that he would help me the best he could. Sometimes he would send me invites to do poetry outside or at other churches. I didn't go to all of them, but I did let him know that I appreciated him. The last event he invited me to was somewhere in Decatur. This was an annual event that usually attracted a big crowd. He told me they were expecting at least 150 people. He wasn't paying me, but I could set up a table to sell my product. I arrived early as usual to set up my table. 20 people showed up. 5 of them were the poets performing. There I was sitting at my table with my product neatly laid out. I think I sold 2 books. It took me 40 minutes to get to the event and 40 minutes to get back home. I'll let you calculate the gas money I spent.

As I was packing up my table, an older lady came over to tell me how impressed she was with my performance. I gave her my business card and headed back home. I felt defeated. I felt like I had wasted my time. This was beginning to be a cycle for me. Driving an hour here and there, only to come back home empty handed.

A few weeks later, I received a phone call from a lady named Sheila. She was with the NAACP. She called me because the lady who I gave my business card to, at the previous event, spoke highly of me. Sheila was looking for a poet to perform at the NAACP banquet, in Clayton County. Talk about favor. Sheila had never heard me perform. She had not seen any of my YouTube videos. She called me based on what someone else had to say about me.

When I arrived at the event, the tables were decorated with such elegance. There were gold chandeliers hanging from the ceiling. The room was full of about 50 round tables, draped in gold table cloths. They had a live band and served a full course meal. I knew the moment I walked in, this was going to be a classy event. I set up my table in the far-right corner. I came prepared with plenty of product and business cards. Slowly, the guest started trinkling in. These were some of the most prestigious black people I've ever seen. They came in wearing fur coats. The men were clean in their tailored suits and bowties. The ladies walked with dignity and poise. About 150 people showed up. I performed one poem and received a standing ovation. I sold a lot of product and passed out a lot of business cards. I praised God all the way home.

Everything we do is a seed. Do not despise the day of small beginnings. Its easy to get discouraged when we don't see the fruits of our labor. Its easy to throw a pity party and just quit. Every time I got on that stage to perform, I performed as if Oprah was sitting in the crowd. Whether it was 5 people or 50, I did it with excellence.

There is so much talent in Atlanta that its easy to get intimidated, if you are not confident in what you do.

This wasn't Oklahoma City, where an open mic list consisted of maybe 5 poets. No, in Atlanta, an open mic event might have 20 poets signed up. They don't pay open mic poets, so unless you're the feature for the night, you won't make any money. Most of the artist walk in with a backpack and hound the audience to buy their stuff. I didn't want to do that. I felt like it would diminish the value of my product. Half of the time I wouldn't even mention that I had product, because there were so many artists in the room. I knew that I had a purpose. I knew that my poetry would speak to the soul of all who heard it. I was confident in who I was and what I brought to the table. Atlanta caught wind and the features started rolling in.

As time progressed, my vision for myself changed. I had to tweak some of the things I put in my magical creation box. I would add things like, going viral on the internet. I put pictures of celebrities that I wanted to meet in there. Kandi Burris, T.I, Tyler Perry and Ellen. I wrote small checks out to myself to build my faith. If there was a pair of shoes that I wanted or article of clothing, I put it in the box. I read my daily affirmations out loud and continued to walk by faith. Remember I still didn't have a job and more money was going out than coming in. I cried many days and nights. My bills in Atlanta were much higher than Oklahoma City. My 401k was starting to run out.

I saw a flier for an all ladies event and decided to go and sign up for the open mic. The room was packed with about 50 women and I could perform 2 pieces. I received a standing ovation. A lady in the crowd approached me about my performance. She was a mystic. She started telling me how powerful I was and that I was going to be successful. She told me some things about myself that only God could have told her. I believed every word she said.

A few weeks later, she messaged me about an opportunity to act in a short film.

"Hey you, my acting coach needs a tomboy to play in a short film. Would you be willing to do it?"

I've never acted before though."

"You can do it. It's like poetry."

"Okay. Let's go."

"Awesome. Text me your number and I'll pass it on."

I sent her my phone number and the next day, the lady called me. She told me the film was about domestic violence and I would be the aggressor. She emailed me the script for the short film and gave me the dates to shoot. I told the lady I didn't know how to act, but again she trusted the word of someone else.

I drove an hour to the location where we would film.

I met the acting coach, the producer, the videographer, the writer and the lady who would be acting with me. They told us to be prepared to be on set for at least 10 hours. We completed the short film in 3 takes.

"Is this your first time acting?" The lady asked.

"Yes ma'am."

"You did an amazing job."

"Are you just telling me that to make me feel good?"

"Listen, if you wasn't good I would tell you that we are going to use someone else. I would tell you to take some acting classes. You did exceptionally well!"

"Thank you."

"We finished in 3 takes. Do you know how rare that is?"

"No ma'am, I don't know anything about acting."

"Girl you got the IT factor."

"Thank you."

I thought about the psychic in Oklahoma City on my way home. Remember she told me that she saw me acting. I had to step out of my comfort zone and trust the process. In doing so, I discovered a new talent and gained more exposure.

After meditating one morning, I sat sipping my coffee, basking in the silence of oneness. Something told me (my intuition) to go online, and check court records in my granny's name. Apparently, there was a probate case opened back in 2014. The case was determining the heirs of her estate to distribute her personal property. The case had been opened for a whole year and I had no idea. After reading through the court dockets, I discovered that my cousin on my daddy's side, was trying to cheat me out of my inheritance. He made a sworn statement to the court stating that my daddy had no living children, which would increase his portion of my granny's estate. My mouth dropped. I couldn't believe my eyes. My cousin knew I was alive and well because he saw me a year earlier at my granny's funeral! I emailed the lawyer who was handling the probate case and I let him have it. I told him who I was, and that his client made a false statement, in attempts to profit off my granny's estate. The lawyer responded:

"Since I do not represent you, I can not give you legal advice. If you are an heir, then you will need to seek separate counsel to change the order determining the heirs that was entered over a year ago."

"Will do." I replied.

I didn't do anything. I knew this was a battle that I would have to fight in the spirit. I didn't have the money to hire a lawyer, but I knew the power of words. I knew that my God was a way maker and he would fight my battles for me. For two months, twice a day, I spoke to that mountain. I said, "I call on the law of justice to work in my life and affairs and it becomes visible now!" I did not waiver. I did not faint. I did not miss a day.

Out of the blue, I received an email from the lawyer stating, "Kendal, you and your brother, have been included in the estate of _____." Please provide a current address for yourself and your brother, so that you may be properly notified of the filings." I replied with my address and a few weeks later, I received a check for $3,000. The case was now closed. People will try to cheat you out of what's yours, but the laws of the universe are working in your favor. You just have to learn how to active them with your words! This was another tangible expression of God reassuring me; I GOT YOU.

I knew the $3,000 would only last me two months, so I started looking for a job. After applying for at least 50 jobs online, I started to worry again. Nobody responded. Not one company. I submitted resumes on every job search website known to man. I even applied directly from the company website. I applied for the city, the government, part time and full time. You name it, I applied for it. Nothing happened. I've had good paying jobs, with longevity. I have never had a problem getting a job. I knew it was a spiritual intervention but why? God knew I was hanging by a thread. He knew my bank account was almost depleted. Why can't I find a job? If he wanted me to follow my purpose and walk in my calling, I would need gas money to get there. Sometimes I would fuss at God. I would stand in the middle my living room and just go smooth off. I was frustrated. I didn't have family in Georgia. I didn't have any friends yet. I was 12 hours from home. Somethings has got to give.

On 12-6-2015 I had a dream. I could hear my mommas voice in my right ear. "Kendal you can fix everything with your name. Your name is Kendal." She continued, "You don't have to worry about anything. I promise everything is going to be alright." Then she said, "I am free now. I am free to travel." I started crying in the dream, saying, "momma I love you." Then I woke up. I tried to make sense of what my momma meant so I googled my name. Kendal means royal valley. A valley is a low area between hills or mountains often with a river running through it. The bible says in John 7:38 Whoever believes in me, as the scripture has said, out of his heart will flow rivers of living water." Even at my lowest, I would always be treated like royalty. My momma was telling me to remember who I am. Remember the power that I have. She reminded me to stay plugged into my source and to go with the flow. Everything will be okay.

I was inspired and disturbed from that dream. Inspired because the message came at a time when I needed encouragement. Disturbed because my momma was still alive. What did she mean by she is free to go? Was she about to die? Was she sick? I called my momma as soon as I woke up.

"Hello."

"Momma."

"You must be dreaming again."

"Yes, are you okay?"

"Yea I'm fine. What's going on?
"Are you sick?"
"I'm alright. Did you have a dream?"
"Yea, I heard you talking to me while I was sleep."
"Oh, well what did I say?"
"You said you was free to go. Free to travel."
"Hmm. I don't know."
"Momma if you sick, you need to go to the doctor."
"I'm alright."
"Alright, I'll let you go back to sleep."
I knew something was going on with my momma, I just didn't know exactly what it is. My momma was like the boy who cried wolf. It was always something wrong with her. We never knew when to take her seriously when she was sick. But if she said she was alright, I just had to take her word for it.

Wednesday night I decided to go to Kat's café to get on the open mic list. After my performance, a lady named Donna came over to me, to tell me how much my poem inspired her. We exchanged business cards and became good friends from then on. She put together a group of poets for a web project and I was fortunate to be a part of it. As time passed, I shared with Donna my difficulty in finding a job. Coincidently, she knew a guy named Pete who was about to retire as president of a marketing company. She called Pete and put in a good word for me. Pete hired me on the spot.

Timing is everything. I can't help but wonder had I not went to Kat's café that night, I would still be looking for a job. Even though it was a part time job, it was better than nothing. Before I could officially start working, I had to take a drug test within 48 hours. I drove 25 minutes to a doctor's office that was closed when I arrived. I wasted gas and became instantly aggravated. I googled the next facility on the list, and it was another 30 minutes in the opposite direction. When I pulled into the parking lot, it was packed. This made me even more agitated because I didn't want to be there all day. I walked in and gave the lady my name. She handed me a clip board to fill out and hand back to her. I waited patiently for her to call my name.

After waiting for about 10 minutes, this older Caucasian lady walked in with her oxygen tank, and sat two seats over from me. She had to be at least 90 years old. The lobby was so quiet, you could hear a pin drop. This lady sat down, and the only thing I could hear was her labored breathing. She was breathing so loud, you could hear her with headphones on. It sounded like a dog and a freight train at the same time. Nobody in the lobby seemed to be concerned with this woman's breathing. They were reading magazines and pre-occupied with their cell phones. I glanced at her, and she was hunched over trying to adjust the oxygen tank. She had tubes in her nose, but she still couldn't breathe. The louder it got, the more painful it sounded. I heard a voice in my inner ear.

"Go pray for her."
I started arguing with God under my breath. I was like, "nah, she don't know me. She gone think I'm weird. I'm not touching her." I heard the voice again.
"Go pray for her."
It sounded like the lion in my dream. After arguing with God, I jumped over to the seat next to me. I asked the lady, "ma'am do you mind if I pray for you?" She looked at me and said, "I would like that very much," as she gasped for air. I didn't want her to think I was freaky, but I knew if I just touched her, she would be healed. I placed

my right hand over her left hand, and bowed my head as if I was praying. I instantly felt a surge of electricity come out of my hand into hers. The palm of my hand felt like a furnace. Her breathing got lighter and lighter and eventually the loud gasping ceased. She looked at me, eyes bucked, in awe and said, "who are you?"

"Do you feel better?"

"I feel much better. Thank you!"

A minute later, the home health aide who brought her to the doctor's office walked in.

"This young lady just healed me." The old lady said.

"That's nice."

The aide checked her oxygen tank and it was empty. She took the tank outside to swap it out. The lady behind the counter called my name and I went to the back room. When I was finished, I walked out of the lobby and waived at the old lady. "Take care now."

When we are intuitively guided, we are always at the right place at the right time. No wonder the first doctor's office was closed. I wasn't supposed to be there. That home health aide was cold and detached. She let that old lady walk in by herself with an empty oxygen tank. I am glad that I was obedient and listened to that voice, because she could have died.

I praised God all the way home. I thanked him for that lady's healing and for using me as a vessel. I thanked him for my new job. I thanked him for constantly reassuring me that everything would be okay. Everything is not always about you. Sometimes God will inconvenience us to get a blessing to someone else. There is a reason why the train is stuck on the tracks when you get to that intersection. There is a reason why your flight is delayed. There's a reason why you can't find your car keys when you're in a hurry. Pay attention to the signs from your angels. They only want the highest and best for you. When you start looking at things from a higher perspective then you will recognize just how blessed you are. God's got you.

I started my new job in February of 2016, but it was only for 25 hours a week. I didn't know how God expected me to survive with that many hours. By this time my 401k had completely ran out. I was getting booked for shows but poetry doesn't pay that much. It wasn't something I could live on unless I had a show every day of the week. I didn't have a support system in Georgia so that interfered with my ability to travel.

I wanted Kory to feel at home in Georgia, so I let some of his friends in the apartments spend the night on the weekends. I wasn't too sure about the oldest boy, but the youngest one was attached to Kory. They were unkept and the clothes they wore were too small. They didn't keep their hair cut and they stayed hungry. I didn't mind feeding them, but they were eating up all our food. After spending the night three weekends in a row, their mother finally came over to introduce herself. I felt it was kind of odd that she waited this long to do so. She was young, and her appearance was disheveled. Her hair was all over the place. She had a scent to her and I don't mean a good one. I could tell she was struggling to provide for the boys. I told her they could stay over anytime.

After she left, I walked to the mailbox to get some fresh air. The mailbox was at the front of the complex, so I had to walk through the parking lot, past the swimming pool, and up the stairs to get there. As I was walking, I noticed a big hawk circling above the parking lot. For some reason it caught my attention. After I grabbed my mail, I headed back to the apartment and the hawk was still circling above. This guy was walking towards me, who I had never seen before. I don't know if he lived in the complex or was just passing through. As I approached him, he looked me in the eye and said, "you see them hawks." It was an eerie experience. It was the way he looked at me that quickened my spirit.

"Yep."

I looked back and the man was gone. The hawk was still circling above. I was trying to make sense of what just happened. Where did the man go? What was the meaning of a hawk? What was it trying to tell me? I googled the meaning of a hawk and it said to keep a close watch on someone or some situation. Hawks are associated with strong visions and seeing things clearly. Seeing hawks also means that you are on the right path in life. Hawks encourage you to study situations thoroughly before making any rash decisions.

A few days later, I was on the phone with a friend talking about life in Atlanta. I was updating her on my new job and how we were barely making ends meet. I looked over at the window seal and there were lady bugs crawling everywhere! I've never seen that many lady bugs in my life. I counted 12 lady bugs. I said, "girl something good is about to happen to me." Lady bugs are a sign of good luck. Not even a minute later, I heard a knock on my door. I answered and there she stood crying. I knew it was some mess. It was the boy's mother. She had both kids with her as they stood with their head hung low.

"Hey what's up?" I asked.

"We just got evicted."

By the look on the boy's face, this wasn't her first rodeo. I didn't know her or her story, but my intuition said the same.

"Aw I'm sorry."

"They told me I had 24 hours to come up with the money and when I came back with the check, all my stuff was outside."

"Wow."

I knew there had to be more to the story, but I just listened to her.

"This is all of our food. You can have it." She says. Next to her stood a tall box of food. Filled to the rim.

"Thank you."

They walked off in tears and I took the food in the house. I had a feeling that wouldn't be the last time I'd hear from her. I didn't know whether to cry for her or be happy about the food. The only thing we had in our cabinet was a box of Ramon noodles. She gave me enough food to fill my refrigerator, my freezer and all my cabinets. I praised God for the food and prayed for her family. The boys went to the same school as Kory. I don't know where they moved to, but I would see them at the bus stop in the morning. In the evening, they would get off the bus and follow Kory home. Kory has so much compassion for people. He would bring home stray cats and stray people all the time.

"Mom can they come in?"

"Yea Kory."

One day turned into a week and the next thing I knew those boys were basically living with us. I told their mother they could come over after school, but she had to pick them up when she got off work. She didn't get off work until 11pm. I let her sleep on my couch for one night and she left a scent on my couch and pillows. I had to throw away the pillows. After picking them up twice, she asked if they could just spend the night, because she was picking them up around midnight. They were interfering with the schedule Kory was on. He was used to going to bed around 10, but we all know when boys get together, there is no sleeping involved. They would be up all night. I noticed a change in Kory's mood. He is an empath, so he would take on the emotions of the boys. That oldest boy never smiled. He had a darkness about him that I didn't like. If they had an attitude, Kory would have one. If they were sad, he would be sad. His grades started dropping and after one phone call from his teacher, I knew something was off.

After a month of her leaving the kids at my house, and not coming to get them, I was fed up. I asked Kory what their last name was, so I could google her. I found court records in Florida that showed she was evicted 3 times! She also had a criminal record for grand larceny and domestic violence. I knew something was fishy about this chic. I texted her and told her I would not be able to keep her kids anymore. She had the audacity to have an attitude, but I didn't let that sway my decision. She picked the boys up around midnight and I never heard from her again. She never thanked me for allowing her kids to stay with me. She tried to play the victim and take advantage of my kindness, but I had to follow my gut. My intuition was on point. Kory was angry with me for not letting the boys stay anymore. I had to explain to him that some people will try to take advantage of you. It is my duty as his mother to protect his spirit from vampires, but he couldn't understand it. A few months later, the oldest boy was arrested for putting his hands on his mother.

I felt bad for those kids. I really did. In the midst of her storm, she was able to be a blessing to me, and I was able to be a blessing to her. I didn't have the money to take care of those kids. Kory and I were barely making ends meet ourselves. I did the best I could with what I had. Our angels can see things from a higher perspective than we can. Sometimes we can get so caught up in our feelings, that we can't see when someone is trying to pull the wool over our eyes. You can't help everybody and I'm okay with that.

In pursuit of my dreams, I started submitting to casting calls for background acting. Eventually I landed a gig on Oprah's hit show, Greenleaf. I was in one of the church scenes playing a member of the congregation. We were on set for 12 hours and I never even saw my face. We got paid $68 for 8 hours plus any overtime. The check was about $100. I landed another background gig for a show called "Not again" staring Letoya Luckett and Wendy Raquel Robinson. As a background actor, you're not allowed to speak to the headliners. It was an honor to be amongst such great talent. Again, we were on set for 12 hours. That check was about $100. I'm not sure how I was supposed to land a gig with actual lines on a hit show, but I was opened minded about it. Background acting just wasn't my thing though.

On 4-10-16 I had a dream that I met a psychic. In the dream, he asked if I was sad. He told me that he saw prosperity in my future and that it was more money than I could pour. He also said that it wouldn't be for a long time because there's a lot to learn, by the time the money comes. He told me it's the type of success that makes you feel guilty but advised me not to feel guilty. I woke up. This was the 3rd prophecy spoken over me from psychics. I had mixed emotions about these prophecies because on one hand I believed them, and on the other hand, it just added to my frustration. Where is this money that I'm supposed to have? Where is this success that seemed so close yet eluded my fingertips? By this time, I'd performed on just about every stage in Atlanta. I've made a good name for myself and doors continued to open for me. However; I was still living paycheck to paycheck. Struggling to make ends meet. Its hard to keep your faith up, when your hungry. Its hard to believe the word of the Lord when you don't have gas money. Deep down I knew that it was the truth. I had my good days and bad days. Sometimes my faith was unmovable and other times I would break down and cry. I had to keep my thoughts positive, remain optimistic and continue to follow my purpose.

I like to think of myself as a non-certified FBI agent. I can be nosey. I know how to find information on anybody and I usually get exactly what I'm looking for. Sometimes its good information and other times not so good. I created a fake twitter account, to keep up with my teenage son, my nieces and nephews. They were at that age where they don't tell you everything that's going on in their life, instead they tweet it! On May **22,** my intuition told me to log into twitter and see what my niece was tweeting about. She tweeted

"OMG not my memaw."

From the time stamp on the tweet, it appeared she posted it in the middle of the night. That tweet felt like a punch in the chest. I called my sister n law and asked her what was wrong with momma? She said, she hadn't heard anything. She told me she would ask my brother and see if he heard anything. None of us knew what was going on. My niece lived with my momma, but she didn't call us to inform us that anything had happened. My sister n law called me back and told me that my momma was in the hospital, and they were headed down there to see her. Like I said before, my momma was like the boy who cried wolf. It was always something wrong with her and we never knew when to take her seriously. This time would prove to be different.

My momma was in a comma. My niece found her on the floor, foaming at the mouth. We don't know how long she had been there before she was found. The doctors said that her organs were shutting down and she wasn't going to make it. There were several things wrong with my momma that played a part in the decline of her health. I reflected on the dream I had of her just 4 months previous, where she said it was time to go. I believe she was sick at the time but didn't want us to know. I also know that my momma was extremely depressed. She wasn't her usual happy self. There were a lot of things going on in her personal life that ultimately affected her standard of living. She was ready to go. Because of my understanding of what happens when we pass, my reaction to this news wasn't as dramatic as everyone else's. The biggest problem I had was working up the courage to tell Kory.

The same day, I took Kory and his friends to the swimming pool. The pool in our complex wasn't open yet so I took them to another apartment complex. Kory could tell something was bothering me.

"Mom what's wrong?"

"Nothing pooda."

"Doesn't look like nothing to me."

"I'm fine."

I sat in the corner of the pool area on a fold out chair and watched Kory swim. He was so happy and free that I just didn't want to tell him about his memaw. I was receiving text messages from family members updating me on the status of moms decline. We stayed at the pool for about 2 hours and headed back to our complex. When we got home, I decided to make some lunch while the boys went outside to play. I tried to keep Kory as busy as possible to give me time to figure out how to bring it up. At 4pm on 5-22-16, I felt a warm impression on the back of my right calf. My leg was so hot, it felt like I was standing in front of a furnace. I instantly knew it was my momma. I knew that she was making her rounds before she took her last breath. I went into my bedroom and sat on the bed. I spoke to my momma out loud. "Moma, I love you. I forgive you. Please forgive me if I've ever hurt you. You are free to go. Please just go." I cried. I yelled. I fussed. I wiped my face and released every bad emotion I had towards my momma. I heard a knock at the door. It was Kory's friend.

"Um, ma'am something is wrong with Kory." He said.

"What? Where is he?"

"He's hallucinating. He doesn't know where he is."

Just as I was about to walk outside, Kory comes to the door.

"Mom I don't know where I am."

"What? What do you mean Kory?"

"I got confused on the stairway. Everything was blurry, and I couldn't see."

"Did you feel the cold feeling?"
"Yes."
I knew it was my momma. She had visited Kory. I didn't want to tell him that she was in the hospital because I didn't want to break his heart. I let him play with his friends for the rest of the day as if nothing had happened. I was still communicating with my family back in Tulsa about her status. I tried to keep myself busy so that I could be strong for Kory. The next day I went to work as usual. My aunt called to tell me that the doctors wanted to have a conference call with us. She couldn't understand why I was at work. What else was I supposed to do? I was 12 hours away. I wasn't making enough money to miss a day of work, and I couldn't help the situation by sitting at home. Later on that evening, the doctors called us on 3 way. He said all of her organs have shut down and the machines were keeping her alive. He said she had no brain activity. I told my aunt that my momma had already left the day before. I told her that she was making her rounds and that she had already visited me and Kory. I told them to let her go. She is already gone.

On May 23rd my momma made her transition to heaven. My brother called me and said, "Momma is gone." And I said, "I know."
I feel like God was preparing me months ago for this. I had time to process my emotions way before they found her passed out on the floor. Now it was time to tell Kory. I sat him down on the edge of the couch. My eyes watery from trying to hold back the tears.
"Pooda I need to tell you something."
"Is it memaw? Did she die?"
"How did you know Pooda?"

"Did she? Was she in the hospital?"
I broke down in tears. He broke down in tears. We held each other on the couch for what felt like an eternity.
"No mom! No! I want my memaw!"
"I know baby. I know."
We rocked back and forth, wrapped in each other's arms. I let him cry until he had nothing left. He stood up, wiped away his tears and went outside to play. He was perfectly fine for the remainder of the day. Four days later, I received a visitation from my momma. As I was asleep, I felt someone place their hand in the palm of my right hand and then squeeze my bicep. I was crying in my sleep saying, "momma don't go!" I woke up.

Since my birthday was June 2nd, I didn't want to have momma's funeral on the same day, so we set it for June 1st. My rent was due in a few days and I only had $68 in my bank account. I didn't know how I was going to pay my rent, let alone get to Tulsa. Luckily, my brother's wife had a family reunion in Atlanta, so she picked up Kory and took him back to Tulsa with her. My brother bought me a plane ticket, and I met Kory in Tulsa the following day. I only spoke to one friend about my financial struggles. She was my accountability partner.

Nobody else knew what my situation looked like. From the outside looking in, I was doing well. I had shows almost every weekend. I kept a positive outlook on my future. I never spoke ill of my situation. I looked like who I said I was. I encouraged people to stay faithful and keep speaking those affirmations over themselves. People admired my diligence to pursue my dreams, but they didn't know the whole story. It looked like I just quit my job and moved to Atlanta. I didn't want to do any of this. I was just following Gods command. If I had never heard that voice, I would still be in Oklahoma. I would be miserable, but I would be financially stable. People came to me to fix their problems not knowing I had problems of my own. Don't forget to check on your strong friend. Sometimes they need encouragement too.

I went to Tulsa with $68 in my bank account and came back with $2,625 in hand. I did not ask anyone for money. Between my family and friends, all of my needs were met. I am eternally grateful of their obedience to sow into my life. If my momma hadn't passed away when she did, I don't know if I would have a place to live. This is Atlanta. They don't just put an eviction notice on your door, they put all of your belongings outside. I saw at least 3 different residents, with their entire apartment outside in the pouring down rain. Atlanta don't play. I have never seen anything like it. I prayed that I would never have to experience it. The homeless population in Atlanta is one of the highest in America. Here I am, the dream chaser. The girl who heard a voice come out of the wall and followed it. The girl who works 25 hours a week and by the grace of God, I have never hit rock bottom. God's got you.

This is what my life looked like for the duration of my time in Atlanta. Every month, someone was paying my bills, giving me money or giving me food. When there was a new moon, I would make a list of 10 things I needed. I wrote down what bill needed to be paid. I would read the list out loud, and put it in my magical creation box. Working 25 hours a week, all of my bills miraculously got paid. When people don't live by faith, its hard for them to comprehend how your doing it. I couldn't explain spiritual things to carnal minded individuals because they couldn't relate to me spiritually. I've had people tell me that I needed to go back to school to get a degree. Others have told me about jobs that are hiring and how easy it is to get on at that job.

I got tired of trying to explain to people that my life is not a normal life. I can apply at jobs all day long, but if God don't want me working there, I won't get the job. That statement alone sounds crazy to people who take credit for their own success. People who don't pray and don't seek God for direction. People who are just existing and not living. It was frustrating to me because I wanted to have a normal life. I wanted to work a 40-hour job and I tried! But I also know when there is a spiritual interference preventing me from living an ordinary life.

That's why you can't share your dreams with everybody. You may have every confirmation from the universe that you're going to be successful, but people who don't have a vision for themselves, surely won't see the vision you have for yourself. They will speak against it and try to talk you out of it. Call you a dreamer and make a mockery of you. You have to stand firm on the direction that God has given you. You have to know without a shadow of a doubt, that his word will not return unto him void.

God has a purpose for me. If I had a full-time job, I couldn't attend some of the events that I did. I've had numerous radio interviews that took place in the middle of the day. I attended conferences that required me to be there at 1pm. I was doing poetry at peoples houses in the middle of the day. I knew what God was doing. I just didn't understand why I had to be so uncomfortable, when I was following his lead.

On June 9th, a friend of mine invited me to a poetry slam taking place in Stone Mountain. I don't like slam competitions because I think it takes away from the pureness of the poem. I don't like the idea of someone judging my poetry. I had no intention of participating in the slam, so I figured what the heck. Might as well get out of the house and go support her. As soon as we walked in, I recognized a lot of the poets. The list to sign up for the competition was almost full. We sat down and waited for the show to start. A few people came up to me and asked was I going to participate, and I told them I didn't like competing. After the third person asked, I knew it was a sign that I was supposed to sign up. The lady who was hosting the show got on the mic and did a last call for poets. There were 18 poets signed up and I was 19 on the list. Someone else signed up and the show started. I had no idea what poems I would do but I gave it my best shot.

There were 3 rounds. I made it threw the first two rounds based on the scores from the judges. The last round was between me and two other poets. I did the poem about my daddy. This time the crowd would decide who the winner is. The judge stood next to one of the finalist, put her hand over his head, and asked the crowd to clap if he should win. The crowd yelled and screamed. She did the same thing for the next person. The crowd clapped. Then she came over to me, put her hand over my head, and asked the crowd if I should win. The crowd went crazy! They yelled, screamed, shouted in an uproar for me. I came in first place out of 20 poets. They handed me $180. I was given a plaque that read "Dopest Performer BPC Poetryfest 2016. My Electricity bill was $120, and I had enough to fill up my gas tank.

I believe my daddy helped me win that slam. I could feel his presence standing behind me the entire time I performed.

My lease was up in July and that meant my rent would increase $100. I reconnected with a friend of mine who had moved to Atlanta, around the same time as I did. She was looking for a place to stay so we thought it would be a good idea for us to be roommates. It would be cheaper for us to split rent in a 3 bedroom than it was for me to stay where I was. I went to the office and applied for a 3-bedroom apartment in the same complex. I loved those apartments and the location, so I didn't want to go anywhere else.

The apartment manager assigned me a three-bedroom apartment across the street. The apartment number was 1304. A few days later, he called to tell me that he needed to change the apartment, because the previous renters would not be out in time. I knew to just go with the flow, so I told him that would be fine. He called me back with the new apartment number 1222. I can't make this stuff up!

Since I'd made so many lists for my magical creation box, I figured I might as well take a stab at finding a companion. Dating is difficult in Atlanta. I knew I was ready to settle down and build a future with someone. However; I was hesitant to get involved with anyone because of my financial situation. I didn't have anything to offer anyone financially. I needed someone who could see past my current situation and see my potential. I also needed someone who wasn't about playing games because I certainly wasn't. I needed someone who didn't want anything from me but would be willing to receive my love with open arms. I love hard and my love aint for everybody.

I prayed and asked my momma and granny if they would find someone for me. On 7-20-16 I made a list. At the top of the paper I wrote, "To my future girlfriend." I wrote down the character traits that were important to me in a mate. I was specific enough to set a standard but not too specific that I would pass up a good thing. So, I didn't write down "she must be 5'3, dark skinned with curly hair." My list was two pages long. She needed to beautiful, in shape, independent, nurturing, spiritual, loyal, faithful, articulate, wise, confident, classy, ambitious, give me space, a good listener etc. I ended the letter with, "I can't wait to meet you. I love you already." I put that letter in my magical creation box and let the universe do what it does.

On 8-8 I happened to be scrolling down my time line on Instagram and I came across this beautiful woman. Her eyes paralyzed me. I felt a quickening in my spirit. She had a little glow behind her eye and I could tell she was an angel. Literally. I heard a voice.

"Message her."

I argued with this voice. (here we go again)

"Nope. I'm not messaging her. She probably got 100 inbox messages from thirsty people trying to get with her."

I scrolled on by. Something wouldn't let me keep scrolling. So, I went back to her picture and checked out her profile. I saw that she was into physical fitness and eating right. She looked kind of young. I couldn't tell if she was in a relationship or not, but I assumed she was. She was too fine to be single. "Message her." I heard it again. But what do I say? I didn't want to sound like everybody else. I didn't want to be elementary and just say Hi. That's annoying. I hit the message button and took a stab at it.

"Well aren't you adorable." I said.

"You are a darling yourself."

I stared at the phone for the longest trying to figure out what I should say next.

"What is your name? I asked.

"Cerita."

"Beautiful name. It fits you."

"Thank you. And I see your name is Kendal."

"Yep that's me."

She told me what she did for a living and I told her I was a full-time artist, with a part time job. I instantly felt insecure having to tell her that. She appeared to be pretty stable. After the usual "get to know you" small chat, I asked her if she dates women.

"No, I date men. There is a certain masculinity that I need."

Note taken.

"Why do you ask?" she asked.

"Well I didn't want to be disrespectful."

"I can't see you being disrespectful."

"You would be surprised at what people say to you in your inbox."

She had to get back to work and I closed that conversation out with the assumption that I would never hear from her again. I didn't want to play that game. If she was used to being with men, I wasn't about to compete. I never reached out to her again and I just checked her off the list. Maybe I heard wrong.

Two days later, she messaged me.

"Good morning Kendal."

I thought to myself, umhmm. We exchanged texts back and forth. She asked me a lot of questions. She told me that she was intrigued with me. She said that I was impressive without trying to impress her. I liked her conversation. She seemed to have a good head on her shoulders. She fit my description of what I wanted in a mate. One day turned into two weeks, and three weeks later she told me that she loved me. The only problem was that she lived in Mobile, Alabama and I was in Atlanta. We decided to meet up half way in Montgomery, Al. She drove a Chevy Silverado truck and I told her I would be in a black Camaro. I had 2 hours to get my thoughts together. I was anxious, nervous and scared all at the same time. We had already exchanged I love you's. What if she didn't look like her pictures? What if our energy collides and we didn't mesh well together? I was about to find out.

I turned left onto Commerce Street in Montgomery. I saw her truck parked, facing the sidewalk. My heart started beating out of my chest. My palms were sweaty. Lord have mercy, what have I gotten myself into? I parked my car about 10 cars down the way. I checked my appearance 3 times before I got out of the car. I made my way up the sidewalk towards her car at a snail's pace. It felt like I was walking into a tunnel and everything around me disappeared. I lost track of time. I didn't hear birds chirping or feel the wind blowing. I was in the twilight zone. Finally, as I approached her vehicle she hopped out of her truck. Grinning from ear to ear, she approached me with the face of an angel. Her pictures did her no justice. She was stunning. Her skin was flawless. She didn't wear any make up. Her toes were polished. Her fingernails were natural and painted pink. She was so tiny. She kissed me on the left cheek, wrapped her arms around my neck and said, "hi baby." My whole body went numb. She was the one. She was comfortable in her skin. She had the cutest gap in her teeth that made me forget my whole train of thought. She grabbed my hand and we walked the streets of downtown like nobody else in the world existed.

Even though she had never been with a woman before, she seemed comfortable with me. We sat down on a bench and she instinctively knew to curl up under me. She looked up at me with those bright eyes.

"I love you."

"I love you too."

I felt like I met her in a past life. Her soul was familiar to me. With her, there was no pain, no arguments, no stress, nothing. Everything with us just flowed and it felt good. It felt right. I looked her in the eye.

"One day you gone be my wife."

"Okay."

We spent the weekend together and it was beautiful. I didn't want to leave her presence. She was funny, energetic and just angelic. I loved how inquisitive she was. There was a pureness to her spirit that is so rare. She had her stuff together and it made me want to get my affairs in order. She was the type of woman that I wanted to make proud. I knew that being with me would be a big problem with her family, but she was willing to take a risk and follow her heart.

On our second date, we met up at Biloxi beach. The moment I hopped out of her truck, I noticed a white feather at my foot. I knew it was a sign from my momma letting me know that she approved of my relationship. This was the first white feather that I had ever found. It solidified any doubts I may have had. I know it sounds like we were moving too fast, but I believe a person knows when they have met the one. Just like you know when you have met the wrong one. It doesn't take a rocket scientist to recognize an angel standing in front of you. We spent half of the day on the beach, and then headed over to a friend's house, so she could meet Kory.

We made it to my friend's house and Rita got acquainted with everybody. I introduced her to Kory, and he smiled. Music was playing, and Kory and his friend were dancing in the middle of the living room. Rita jumped up without hesitation and started showing the boys that she could do the latest moves too. Everybody shouted, and the boys threw their hands up and just walked off. It was funny. I knew at that moment she was the missing piece to our puzzle. I was relieved that Kory was so fond of Rita because if he didn't like her, I wouldn't be able to build a future with her. I looked back over that list I made to manifest my mate. She was everything I asked for and more. I've made about 3 lists for the type of partner I wanted, and each time I would meet someone that had those traits. The problem is, I neglected to say, I didn't want a crazy person! Each time I tweaked the list, a new person would appear. I finally got it right. Be careful what you ask for because you will exactly that. Be detailed in your asking. Ask and it is given.

By November, Rita had put her house on the market, and we were planning our future together. On her off days, she would drive 5 ½ hours to Atlanta just to be with me. Every single week. She is the most selfless human being I have ever met. She put me and Kory's needs before her own. I told her about my financial issues and she said, "it's okay baby I got you. I will never let you fail." Every two weeks she would ask me how much money

I needed for my bills and she paid them. She has never ever asked me for anything. She believes in my dreams. The amount of money I had or lack thereof, was never an issue. She loved me. She caught a lot of slack with her family for choosing to be with me. People have disowned her. They have shunned her. The ones closest to her, threw her away like discarded trash, and it breaks my heart. I've watched her cry many tears. I warned her in the beginning that this could happen, but she was tired of living for everybody else. I admire her bravery. I admire her strength to stand up for what she believes in. She is my little angel. For every person who disowned her, she gained another, with my friends and family. They love her just like they love me. My kids call her more than they call me. They absolutely adore her. Its funny how people will hate you based on their religious beliefs that are supposed to be centered around love. If your religion teaches you to treat people different because of their sexuality, nationality, gender or religion then you my friend are in the wrong religion. Love is my religion.

On 11-25-16 I had a visitation from my mother. She was young and healthy. Her voice was peaceful. I asked her if she would forgive me for being mad at her and I told her I was sorry. She said, "Yes I forgive you." Then she said, "make sure you learn all of your lessons while on earth, because once you cross over you don't get those same lessons." I said "okay". Then I told my momma how hard it's been for me lately. She said, "Things are about to get better." I asked her could she help me while I'm on this side and she told me that she would. I woke up.

I believe in my heart that my momma picked Rita for me. I know that she did. I know she wasn't too fond of same sex relationships when she was alive. However; once you cross over to the other side, there is no judgement. Its all about unconditional love. I know that my momma just wants the highest and best for me. I believe it was her voice that told me to send Rita a message. She knew exactly what I needed and who needed me. My life has been better since the moment I laid eyes on her. She adds value to my life. She is heaven sent. I will do everything in my power to show her how much I appreciate what she has done for me. She literally saved my life.

The last day of 2016, I decided to call a psychic. A friend gave me her information. Her name was Uversa Oumbajuah. She was based out of New York. I was told she was the real deal and I needed clarity about my 2017. 2016 was not nice to me and I was tired of struggling financially. Something has got to give. She told me that I needed to revamp my look and take photos in all black. She said she could see many opportunities coming my way. She told me that I would be asked to write something. A book, a play, a blog or something. Whatever this thing was I was to write, she said it would sustain my livelihood. She said she could see me quitting my job. She saw me moving. She saw me getting married. She told me that I would be acting and that I would be very successful. She also told me to get my literature in order and to prepare for a change in March.

I already had 4 books. I haven't been inspired to write a book since 2011. I thought to myself, what could I possibly write that would sustain my livelihood? Why can't the books I've already written sustain me? (laughing but serious). This is the umpteenth time I've been told that I would be successful, but my pockets still didn't match the prophecy. I feel one step closer to it though. I can feel it in my bones. Rita's house had been up for sale since

November and still no offers. On the last day of March, an offer was put on the house and it sold! The psychic was right.

We sat down and made a new list for our future home together. We wrote down the amount of square footage we needed, hardwood floors, 3 bedrooms, 2 bath etc. We wrote down the mortgage payment we could pay and a good school district for Kory. We didn't put a location because I wanted to stay open to wherever God lead us. We signed the letter and put it in our magical creation box. My lease would end in July, so we didn't have that much time to look.

More opportunities started rolling in. I was getting booked for shows at least two weekends out of the month. My book sales increased. My name was buzzing around the city. Things were starting to look up for the kid. One weekend, I had a show at the Calabar & Grill in Stone Mountain. The place was packed. The energy was good. We had a DJ playing some good music. The drinks were circulating, and the poets were dope. I sat in the back the whole night until it was my time to perform. I noticed this man on the dancefloor, dancing by himself. He appeared to be tipsy but very happy. He was having a jolly good time all by himself. Finally, they called me up on stage and I performed 3 pieces. As I walked off the stage, this man came over to me and hugged me tight. I was hesitant because I could tell he was tipsy. He held me like he was my daddy. When he let go, I said thank you and proceeded to the back of the room. He followed me and sat down on the coffee table in front of me. I didn't think much of it because I meet weird people all the time at my shows. No biggie. He turns around, looks me in the eye and says, "You the one."

"Thank you sir."

"You the one."

"Thank you."

"That stuff you saying comes from the heart. These other poets aint talkin about nothin!"

"Okay."

"You don't know who I am do you?"

"No sir."

He appeared to be frustrated that I didn't know who he was. He stood up and looked at me and said. "You the one." Then he sat back down. By this time, I'm like ok, am I supposed to know who this man is.

"What's your name?" I asked.

"Kirk."

I pulled out my phone, went to Facebook, and typed that name in. There was no Kirk on my list. How was I supposed to know who he was? He stood up again, looked at me and said, "I'm proud of you." And walked off.

I was so perplexed by what just happened. This man was so passionate about me, yet I didn't know who he was. It wasn't until I got home, and told Rita about it, that I figured out what just happened.

"Baby that sounds like your daddy."

"OMG! It sure does! That's why he kept saying, you don't know who I am do you?"

"Yep, that was your daddy."

My daddy's name is Curtis. In that moment, my daddy visited me in the form of another person. I wrote a poem about my daddy a few years ago titled, "I wonder if he's proud of me." My daddy in the form of that man, held me so tight. He told me that he was proud of me and walked off. He even sounded like my daddy when he would be drunk, slurring the same way. Hebrews 12:2 Do not forget to show hospitality to strangers, for some who have done this have entertained angels without realizing it.

In May, I felt a shift in my spirit. I felt like I was about to transition into a better life for myself, so it was time that I release the old, to prepare for the new. I took advantage of the full moon, May 10th to release the things, people and places that no longer served my highest good. I wrote down the names of the people who I held animosity towards. I wrote down emotions that I needed to release. The list included the names of exes, family members, friends, enemies etc. I read it out loud and put it in my magical creation box. It was time to let it all go! My hair was tied to my past relationships, unhealthy emotions and unhealthy attachments. Hair holds energy and I knew that it was holding me back spiritually.

After 10 years of growing dreadlocks, I did the big chop and then BAM! I went viral. The barber posted the before and after picture on Instagram and before I knew it, every natural hair page had shared it. It was on blogs, Instagram, Facebook and twitter. One page alone had over 40,000 likes. The last time I checked, the picture had a total of over 100,000 likes. All because of a haircut. There is power in letting go! The last four digits of my barber's phone number is **2292**. The psychic was spot on about revamping my look. She was spot on about something happening in March. Rita's house sold. Doors magically started opening for me. Opportunities just fell in my lap. My book sales were the highest they had ever been. So far, everything she said would happen did.

For my birthday, Rita traded in her truck, to get me a Jeep Wrangler. She knew that was my dream car. Without me having to ask, she sacrificed her own truck for my happiness. It was a 2017 limited edition. The Jeep had 8 miles on it, with the plastic wrap still on the seats. Remember my magical creation box? I put that Jeep in the box in 2014. 3 years later, God granted my wish. All you have to do, is write down your request, and put it in the box. How and when it will come is not your concern. Ask and it is given.

Since neither of us wanted a wedding, we decided to go ahead and make it official. I called 3 different counties in Georgia to see what the process was to get a marriage license. One county would give you the license but you had to bring your own official. The other only performed ceremonies on certain days. We decided to go to Cobb county, because they would give us the license and perform the ceremony on the same day. When we arrived at the courthouse, I asked the clerk for directions. She said all ceremonies would take place on the 3rd floor. I looked at the board on the wall and sure enough; Room 322 was where we got married. Now if that wasn't a confirmation I don't know what is. We got married on June 28th. We chose this day because 2 was obviously my number and 8 is the day that I messaged her on Instagram. 8 is also the number of abundance and prosperity.

We were deep into the house buying process by this time. We already had our pre-approval letter, so we knew how much we could afford. At first, I was stuck on living in the same neighborhood as our apartments, because I'm not good with change. I had gotten used to that area and I knew the school districts were great. We found two houses in that area that we really liked. They were in our price range and we felt good about them. The first house we loved it so much we put a bid on it the same day. The next day someone else outbid us and we lost that house. The second house, we liked just as much. The same thing happened! Within 2 days we were outbid. We started to get frustrated with the market in Georgia. The houses were going the same week they were posted online. Every house we bid on we lost. I knew that my angels were just looking out for us. I told Rita, I didn't want nothing that wasn't for me. We stayed optimistic and expanded our territory.

I decided to step completely out of my comfort zone and look more towards the South. We found a house online that had been on the market for **22** days with no offers. A house with no offers in Georgia for that amount of time was unheard of. Rita wasn't impressed with the outside of the house, but I told her I had a good feeling about it. I convinced her that we should at least check it out. The house was an hour away from where my apartment was. We drove out there in the rain and waited for the agent to show up. She finally arrived to let us in and we loved it. Except for the painfully bright colors on the walls, the house was in tip top shape. Some old couple had been living there and decided to retire and travel the world. The house had everything we wrote down on our list, in our magical creation box. From the square footage to the patio, it was perfect.

We put a bid on the house and got it the same day! We didn't realize until after we put a bid on the house, that the zip code was 30**228**. When it was time to move in, I found a piece of duct tape, stuck on the inside of the garage floor. Written on the tape in black marker, were the numbers **222**. I don't know why someone would write those numbers on a piece of tape. We did not see that tape on the garage floor when we looked at the house. Not only did we get the house, we did not have to compete for the house. Not only did we not have to compete for the house, but we got it for $15,000 less than the asking price. When God has a blessing with your name on it, you won't have to compete for it. You don't have to fight for what's already yours. Your job is to make your request. Believe that it is possible. Speak it into existence. Visualize it as if its already yours. Then wait on it. You have to be in vibrational alignment with what you're asking for. If you ask for something and doubt that you deserve it. You won't get it. If you ask for something but can't keep your thoughts positive, you won't get it. To be in vibrational alignment means to see, feel, speak, think and act as if it is yours! You have to change your thoughts and sometimes your circle of friends to get what you want. If you want something different you have to do something different than you've been doing.

Walking by faith is by no means for the weak or weary. I tell people all the time, its like driving in a dense fog with headlights on. The only thing you can see is what's in front of you. There's no way you will know what's going to happen the next minute or the next hour. You must completely surrender yourself to the will of God. You have to know without a shadow of a doubt that he will not let you fail. Its hard. There will be times when you'll be tempted to quit and go back to the life you've always known. But where has that gotten you? That dead-end job and those miserable friends you've been hanging around. The sexless, miserable marriage you've been stuck in for years. How's that working for you? Don't you want a more meaningful life? Don't you want to live a life full of purpose and not just existing? Surely God didn't put us on this earth to work a 9-5 that we hate, go home to a spouse we don't like, and live in a poverty-stricken neighborhood. No! We are co-creators in this universe. The bible says are ye not Gods? Luke 10:19 says, I have given you authority to trample on snakes and scorpions and to overcome all the power of the enemy; nothing will harm you. He didn't say some things will harm you. He said NOTHING! Stop acting like a victim and be the champion that you are! Its time out for blaming your childhood. Yes, I know you've had it hard. I know you've been living from paycheck to paycheck, and you can't see the light at the end of the tunnel. I know you've been abused and left for dead. I know your family doesn't understand you and you've been judged for the way you love. That is no reason for you to give up. You have to stop blaming everybody else and take responsibility for the bad decisions you made. You can't change the past, but you can change your thoughts today for a better tomorrow.

The psychic told me that I would be asked to write something that would sustain my livelihood. God told me to write this book on December 11, 2017. This book will be on the New York times best sellers list. This book will change the lives of all who read it. This book is going to sustain my livelihood. If you don't get nothing else from this book, just remember that God's got you!

ABOUT THE AUTHOR

Kendal S. Turner is an Atlanta based Spoken word artist, Motivational speaker, Author, Print model and Actress. After graduating from Booker T. Washington High School in Tulsa, OK and a brief stint at Dillard University in New Orleans, LA, Kendal began a journey that lead her to be a beacon of light for the hopeless. From tragedy to triumph, Kendal became an internationally acclaimed author and poet.

Kendal has taken the responsibility of being a phenomenal woman to the next level. In addition to three inspiring books of poetry, "Broken Yet Sustained by God," "Anatomy of the Soul" and "Epiphany," Kendal has also published a page turning autobiography. "Thick Skin" is a gritty, in-your-face autobiography detailing her accounts of rape, abuse and sexual identity crisis that Kendal wrote to not only free herself from the bondage of past hurt, but also to guide others through their journey of healing.

Spinach
greens ō turkey
string beans
zuchunni
cabbage
carrotts

arms-17
chest 60
waist 61
thighs 38